WORLD WAR I
Love Stories

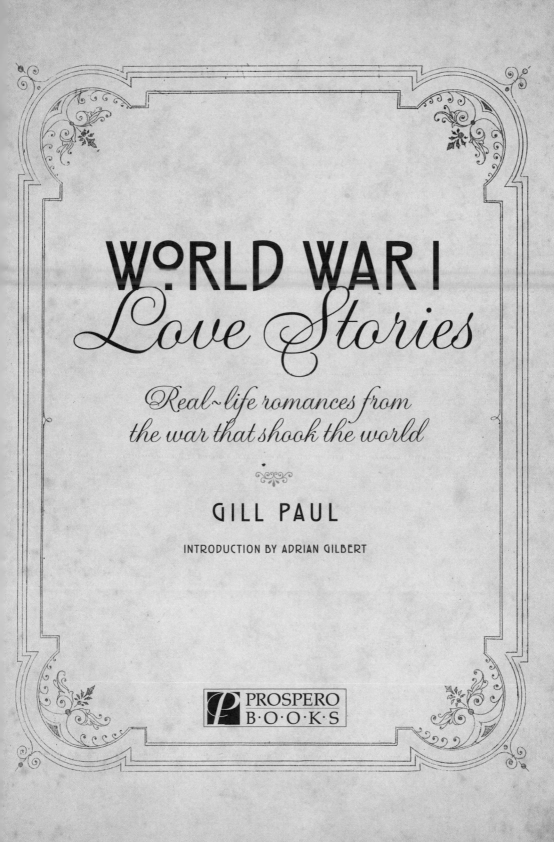

WORLD WAR I
Love Stories

Real~life romances from
the war that shook the world

·

GILL PAUL

INTRODUCTION BY ADRIAN GILBERT

PROSPERO
B·O·O·K·S

For my wonderful mum and dad

Published by Prospero Books,
by arrangement with
Ivy Press

This book was conceived, designed, and produced by
Ivy Press
210 High Street, Lewes,
East Sussex BN7 2NS, U.K.
www.ivypress.co.uk

Creative Director Peter Bridgewater

Publisher Susan Kelly

Art Director Wayne Blades

Senior Editor Jayne Ansell

Designer Andrew Milne

Picture Researcher Katie Greenwood

Cover images: Courtesy of Jeff Staley;
Getty Images/De Agostini Picture Library.

ISBN-13: 978-155-267-915-9

Prospero Books
468 King Street West, Suite 500
Toronto, Ontario M5V 1L8
Canada

Manufactured in China
Color origination by Ivy Press Reprographics

10 9 8 7 6 5 4 3 2 1

CONTENTS

BELOW

*A map illustrating the global
nature of the 1914–18 conflict,
with the major European powers
drawing upon the resources of
their overseas empires.*

SUPPLEMENT TO THE WATCHMAN, NOVEMB

THE BLOOD-RED W

MAP SHOWING TERRITORY OF THE EARTH
DIRECTLY AFFECTED BY THE GREAT WAR

COUNTRIES	POPULATION	PEACE STRENGTH	WAR STRENGTH
British Empire	435,000,000	542,500	1,276,000
Russian Empire	166,250,000	1,290,000	6,500,000
France and Colonies	98,850,000	720,000	3,280,000
Germany	79,054,000	870,000	4,430,000
Japan	67,142,000	250,000	1,200,000
Austria-Hungary	51,340,000	390,000	1,610,000
Turkey	31,000,000	700,600	1,500,000
Belgium	7,432,000	45,000	400,000
Serbia and Montenegro	4,500,000	32,000	329,000
TOTALS	940,568,000	5,339,500	19,525,000

Red shows territory involved in war

*White shows neutral territory with a
population of 579,582,000*

Introduction

by Adrian Gilbert

ABOVE
A US Army machine-gun team prepares for action on the Western Front. By 1918, America was making an important contribution to the Allied war effort.

THE ROAD TO WAR

When a European war broke out in 1914, most military experts believed a resolution to the conflict would be quick and decisive. None had any idea that it would lead to more than four years of unrelenting attritional conflict and the deaths of as many as 16 million people from around the world.

The traditional rivalries among the major nations of Europe intensified in the latter part of the 19th century, fueled by the emergence of Germany as the major economic and military power on the Continent. And yet Germany felt deeply aggrieved by its inability to take a significant share in the vast colonial expansion in Africa and Asia, led by Britain and France. This frustration encouraged the German emperor, Kaiser Wilhelm II, and his government to issue threats of military action that alarmed the other European states. German policy consisted mainly of threats rather than action, but designed to antagonize other European nations—such as supplying arms to the Boers during Britain's war against the Boers.

France, humiliated by Germany during the Franco-Prussian War (1870–71), formed an alliance with Russia for mutual protection against Germany. For its own part, Germany turned to Austria-Hungary to create a competing military alliance, known as the Central Powers. The alliance system was inherently dangerous, however, as an attack by one nation on another was likely to lead to a general European war. Britain had traditionally kept out of direct involvement in such treaty obligations, but Germany's decision to build a powerful fleet and challenge Britain's position as the world's leading naval power pushed Britain toward support for France and Russia.

International tensions increased further with ill-judged German interventions in Morocco, but the real impetus for war lay in the

ABOVE
Kaiser Wilhelm II, the autocratic and often bellicose ruler of Germany.

OPPOSITE
The Archduke Franz Ferdinand and his wife, Sophie, prepare to make the car journey that ended in their assassination.

rivalry of Austria-Hungary and Russia over control of the Balkans. The collapse of the Turkish empire in the region had led to the emergence of new independent states with predominantly Slav populations. Among these was Serbia, openly antagonistic to Austria-Hungary and its control over the Slav province of Bosnia. Russia, already hostile toward Germany and Austria-Hungary, felt a sense of kinship with its fellow Slavs in Serbia.

The assassination on June 28, 1914, of Archduke Franz Ferdinand, heir to the throne of Austria-Hungary, by Gavrilo Princip, a Bosnian Serb nationalist, led Austria-Hungary to declare war on Serbia exactly a month later. This localized decision had swift and far-reaching consequences, as Russia mobilized its army in support of Serbia. On August 1, Germany went to war against Russia, and two days later declared war on France. On August 3, German troops marched through neutral Belgium, as part of their offensive against the French. The following day, Britain, fearful of Germany's military domination of Europe, came out in support of Belgium by declaring war on Germany.

SHOTS HEARD AROUND THE WORLD

In June 1914 Archduke Franz Ferdinand, heir to the throne of Austria-Hungary, made an official visit to Bosnia, which had been incorporated into the Austro-Hungarian Empire in 1908. The Black Hand, a Serbian-supported terrorist group, planned to assassinate the Archduke as part of its campaign to take Bosnia out of Austrian control and into a union with Serbia. As Franz Ferdinand and his wife drove through the Bosnian capital of Sarajevo on June 28, they were mortally wounded by shots fired by Gavrilo Princip, a 19-year-old Bosnian-Serb nationalist. This brazen challenge to Austria-Hungary's authority in the Balkans led eventually to a declaration of war against Serbia on July 28, 1914.

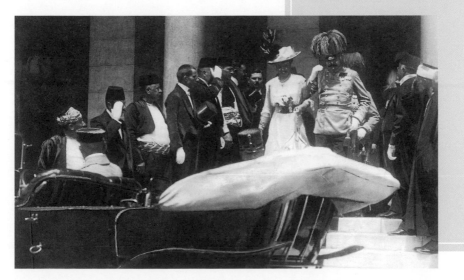

THE BATTLES OF 1914

In August 1914 Germany deployed 1,450,000 soldiers on its western borders, organized into seven armies. Their task was to smash the opposing French forces with the utmost rapidity, and after achieving victory in the West, to turn eastward to deal with the Russians. Subsequently known as the Schlieffen Plan, the German strategy in the West called for its three large northern armies, some 750,000 men, to advance through Belgium and outflank the French, who in theory would be held in position by the other four armies in the south. The French plan, meanwhile, comprised a simple advance into German territory.

Throughout most of August the German strategy went very much as its commanders intended. The French assaults were repulsed with heavy losses while the three attacking German armies advanced through Belgium and into northern France, inflicting a series of defeats on the French, Belgian, and British Allied forces. The Allies were forced to retreat, and, at one point, German cavalry patrols were little more than 20 miles from the outskirts of Paris. The French government fled the capital for Bordeaux.

Fortunately for the Allies, General Joseph Joffre, the French commander-in-chief, quickly realized that his offensive on the Franco-German border had been a failure. Demonstrating great

ABOVE
General Joseph Joffre, whose foresight and determination helped repel the German offensive in the West in 1914.

RIGHT
German infantrymen hold a line of trenches along the River Aisne in 1914. It was on the Aisne that entrenchments first became common in the war on the Western Front.

resolution in this moment of crisis, he reorganized his battered forces and instigated a daring counter-attack against weak points in the German advance. The German commander, General Helmuth von Moltke, was shocked by the strength of the French attacks along his now overextended front, and on September 8 he ordered a general retreat away from Paris.

The Germans managed to retire to a good defensive position on high ground along the River Aisne. Once there they constructed strong defenses that brought Allied progress to a halt. The devastating firepower of the latest weapons—especially machine guns and artillery—made movement in the open virtually impossible; to survive men now had to go underground. As a consequence, from late October onwards, lines of trenches were dug along the entire Front, stretching 450 miles from the Swiss border to the North Sea.

While Germany was making its main thrust against France in the West, it adopted a defensive position in the East. The large, cumbersome Russian armies marched slowly into East Prussia, but on August 26 were trapped by smaller yet more mobile German forces around the village of Tannenberg. In a four-day encirclement battle, the Russian 2nd Army was virtually annihilated. The Germans then turned east and inflicted a second major defeat on the Russians at the Battle of the Masurian Lakes.

These severe defeats at the hands of the Germans notwithstanding, the Russians fared better against Austria-Hungary in the south. An Austrian advance was caught in the flank, forcing the Austrians to retreat in confusion and in the process causing the loss of Austria-Hungary's eastern province of Galicia and some 350,000 men. The Austrian invasion into Serbia was also repulsed with heavy losses. The Germans were shocked at the poor performance of their ally, and were forced to send reinforcements to bolster the wavering Austrian line.

HELP FROM EMPIRE

Britain had the great advantage of being able to call upon its empire and various dominions to provide forces in the war against the Central Powers. South African and Nigerian troops took part in the campaigns against the Germans in Africa, while India supplied the bulk of the men fighting the Turks in the Middle East. Australian and New Zealand soldiers served with distinction at Gallipoli before their transfer to France, where they joined the Canadians on the Western Front. Their participation confirmed the unique contribution of the British self-governing dominions to the war, and in the process helped develop a sense of separate national identity that would lead to the full independence of these countries within the Commonwealth.

THE WIDENING WAR

World War I began as a purely European conflict but the fighting was soon to spread around the globe. New theaters of war emerged as countries far from Europe found themselves inexorably sucked into the great conflict.

Britain's naval supremacy spelled doom for Germany's now isolated overseas colonies in Africa and the Pacific, which soon fell to the Allies. The one exception was German East Africa, where the Germans under Colonel (later General) Paul von Lettow-Vorbeck continued to fight a skillful guerrilla campaign until news reached them of armistice negotiations in November 1918.

Turkey, which had strong military links with Germany, joined the Central Powers in October 1914 and immediately attacked Russia in the Caucasus region, but to little effect. Bulgaria also joined the Central Powers, while Italy and

Romania went to war on the Allied side. Of these states, Turkey was the most important, its empire stretching across Arabia and most of the Middle East, potentially threatening Allied supply links through the Suez Canal and British oil interests in the Persian Gulf. But to the Allies, Turkey also seemed to offer an opportunity to bypass the trench deadlock on the Western Front.

The Allies intended to seize the Dardanelles—the narrow strait that connects the Aegean Sea to the Sea of Marmara—and then push on to Constantinople, modern-day Istanbul. An Anglo-French amphibious force containing large numbers of Australian and New Zealand troops, landed on the Gallipoli peninsula on April 25, 1915, as a first step to seizing the Dardanelles. Turkish resistance was fierce and, despite heavy reinforcement, the Allies were never able to break out of their bridgeheads. At the end of 1915, the Allies abandoned the operation and withdrew from Gallipoli. Further Allied offensives in Palestine and Mesopotamia (modern Iraq) were also repulsed with heavy losses.

Germany had built a powerful fleet in the years leading up to World War I, but was unable to effectively challenge the British Royal Navy on the high seas; apart from an inconclusive encounter at the Battle of Jutland in May 1916, it spent most of the war in the safety of home waters. The Germans had more success with their U-boat submarine war against British merchant shipping until British countermeasures reduced the German undersea threat from mid-1917 onwards. During the U-boat campaign, however, many American ships had been sunk, and in April 1917 this persuaded the US to go to war against Germany, tipping the military balance decisively in favor of the Allies.

German Submarine Crew Captured by U. S. Destroyers

THIS SUBMARINE WAS DESTROYED IN A FIGHT WITH U. S. DESTROYERS FANNING AND NICHOLSON, NOV. 24, 1917. THE CREW SURRENDERED, BUT THEIR VESSEL SANK SO RAPIDLY THAT THEY HAD TO SWIM TO THE FANNING.

OFFICERS AND CREW OF GERMAN U-BOAT 58, CAPTURED BY AMERICAN DESTROYERS, BEING TAKEN TO WAR PRISON CAMP, FORT McPHERSON, GA., UNDER GUARD OF U. S. MARINES.

ABOVE
German U-boats posed a major threat to Allied shipping until the summer of 1917. In this illustration, a German U-boat is sunk by US warships (top) and its surviving crew marched into captivity (below).

OPPOSITE
A camp occupied by Australian and New Zealand Army Corps (ANZAC) troops at Gallipoli in 1915. Despite their best efforts, the Allies were never able to break out of their beachheads.

THE WESTERN FRONT, 1915–17

As the war entered its second year, the Allies prepared to conduct a series of offensives on the Western Front designed to expel the Germans from northern France and Belgium. During 1915 French attacks in the Champagne region and British attacks in Artois were made with the greatest determination, but territorial gains were minimal and casualties heavy. The Germans, focusing on operations on the Eastern Front, successfully remained on the defensive in the west, although a limited attack was made against the Allies at Ypres in April 1915, where poison gas was used effectively for the first time.

In February 1916 the Germans launched a mass offensive against the French around the fortress of Verdun. The German commander's intention was not to achieve a breakthrough but "to bleed France to death" by attacking a sector of the line the French would feel forced to defend, regardless of loss. The French were indeed determined to hold the key position of Verdun and casualties were heavy, but the Germans found that they were losing troops at the same rate as their enemy. When the battle stuttered to a close in December, both sides had suffered over a third of a million casualties each.

In the summer of 1916, the British took the lead in a combined Franco-British offensive on the Somme. The opening of the attack, on July 1, was a disaster for the inexperienced British forces, which suffered nearly 60,000 casualties on that one day alone. Subsequently, British tactics improved and steady gains were made against the Germans, but, as at Verdun, the Somme became a byword for slaughter. As the winter brought the battle to a close, total casualties on both sides amounted to more than a million men.

BELOW
Heavily laden British troops advance over a shattered battlefield on the Western Front. The British took a key role alongside their French ally in fighting the Germans.

During 1917, renewed French and British offensives on the Western Front again failed to produce the hoped-for results. The failure of the French campaign in Champagne led to mutinies within the French army, while the British attack at Passchendaele foundered in the Flanders mud.

The trench deadlock seemed impossible to resolve, although great efforts were made to find new ways or machines to break through the enemy lines. Poison gas was developed on both sides, but its effects were diminished by the introduction of gas masks for the trench-bound infantry. Then the British developed the tank, able to cross the mud of no-man's-land and break into the enemy's trenches. When used in a massed formation at the Battle of Cambrai in November 1917 they achieved some success, but ultimately they were too unreliable to become a war-winning weapon.

More obvious progress was made in the air. The spindly machines of 1914, used for reconnaissance alone, became greatly improved and were used in an increasing number of ways: to correct the accuracy of long-range artillery, to photograph enemy positions, to shoot down enemy aircraft, and to bomb enemy positions and cities far behind the lines. But in the end, the war would be won or lost on the ground. As 1917 drew to a close, all the main armies were suffering from profound weariness, with little prospect of victory in sight.

BELOW
The Allies used the latest technology in an attempt to break the deadlock on the Western Front, including aircraft (below) and tanks (bottom), this example firing one of its two six-pounder guns.

THE WAR IN THE EAST

In 1915, as Germany went over to a defensive strategy in the West, reserve forces were released for service on the Eastern Front. German reinforcements sent to Galicia to help the armies of Austria-Hungary would now form the spearhead of a major offensive into Polish Russia. In May 1915 an Austro-German force broke through enemy lines at Gorlice-Tarnów, taking the Russians completely by surprise. The Central Powers made massive gains, pushing nearly 300 miles forward into Russian territory and inflicting up to two million casualties on the Russians, most of whom were prisoners.

To any other nation, such a defeat would have been a mortal blow. However, Russia not only survived but, with the accelerated development of its military industries, prepared for offensive operations in the following year. Accepting a Franco-British request for action—to relieve pressure on Verdun—the Russians opened their offensive in June 1916. Commanded by Russia's most able commander, General Alexei Brusilov, four Russian armies broke through the Austrian defenses, in response to which the Germans rushed reinforcements to the Front to stem the Russian attack. Unfortunately for Brusilov, he lacked the support of other Russian generals, and the offensive ground to a halt in September.

BELOW
Russian infantry pose beside two Maxim machine guns. The Russian Army endured great hardships and suffered terrible casualties, so that by the summer of 1917 it was on the point of collapse.

The severe winter of 1916–17 caused serious famine throughout Russia, which combined with five million military casualties produced rising unrest in Russia's major cities. In March 1917, against a background of mass demonstrations and the breakdown of discipline within the army and police, Tsar Nicholas II was deposed and a provisional government appointed in his place. The new government continued military operations against Germany, but its authority was challenged by left-wing groups, whose demands for "peace and bread" met with a ready response from the war-weary peasants and soldiers.

After the failure of a Russian offensive in July 1917, the army began to disintegrate, with the Germans driving deeper into Russia and meeting little opposition. In November 1917 the provisional government was overthrown by the Bolshevik faction of the leftist Social Democrats. The new government, under the leadership of V. I. Lenin and Leon Trotsky, immediately sued for peace. On December 15, 1917—to the dismay of the Western Allies—an armistice agreement was signed at Brest-Litovsk, followed by a formal peace treaty in the new year.

The bulk of Germany's divisions could now be redeployed for action on the Western Front. Germany had undoubtedly achieved a great success in the east, but overall the war was not going in its favor. The blockade led by the British Royal Navy was beginning to take effect, depriving the country of essential foodstuffs and vital war materials. Germany's two main allies, Austria-Hungary and Turkey, were also being systematically ground down by Allied material superiority. Worse still, growing numbers of US troops were starting to arrive in France, and by mid-1918 would be ready to make a serious contribution to the Allied cause. The German High Command prepared for one last great offensive in the West.

Russians Who Have Administered Affairs Under Revolutionary Regime

M. JOFFE, one of the signers of the Brest-Litovsk Treaty and afterward Ambassador from the Bolshevik Government to Berlin.

LEON TROTZKY, Minister of War, and leader of the ultra-radical element of the Bolsheviks. In 1919 he arrested his associate, Lenine.

NIKOLAI LENINE, Bolshevist Premier of the Soviet Government until arrested by his associate, Trotsky, in 1919.

MICHAEL TEREITCHENKO, Minister of Finance in First Provisional Government, organized after downfall of the monarchy; later Foreign Minister.

PAUL MILYUKOV, University Professor and Minister of Foreign Affairs in the First Provisional Government.

EROIG TCHITCHERIN, Bolshevist Minister of Foreign Affairs, who caused the arrest of Foreign Consuls in Moscow, 1919.

ABOVE
Some of the key figures in the Russian Revolution, including the two Bolshevik leaders, Vladimir Lenin (center) and Leon Trotsky (top right).

DEFEAT OF THE CENTRAL POWERS

The great German offensive in the West was launched on March 21, 1918, against a section of the line held by the British. Supported by the heaviest bombardment of the war—nearly 10,000 guns, howitzers, and trench mortars—the Germans spearheaded the attack with elite "storm troops" trained in trench infiltration tactics. Outnumbered, the British were unable to hold the German advance and fell back over a wide front, with some German units penetrating to maximum depth of 40 miles. But after a week the German assault began to weaken, just as Franco-British reinforcements were being rushed to the points of gravest danger.

*BELOW
A map of the Western
Front in 1918. The two
broken dotted lines show
initial German advances
in March through to June;
however, by August Allied
troops had regained
ground, as a shift of
the (thicker) battle
line demonstrates.*

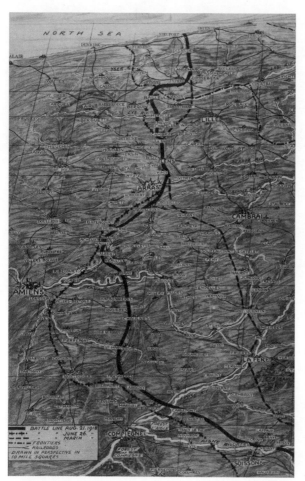

The Germans launched two further attacks in April and May, but despite early successes they, too, failed to break the Allied will to fight. The Germans were now exhausted. In August 1918 the Allies went over to the offensive and, supported by fresh American divisions, they began to push the Germans back to their homeland. This time, the Allied advance could not be halted and by the end of September the German High Command reluctantly accepted that the war was lost.

Germany's plight was made worse by the knowledge that Turkey and Austria-Hungary were also on the point of collapse. The British had defeated the Turks in Mesopotamia and Palestine, and, with the fall of Bulgaria, Constantinople was now under threat. On October 30, 1918 Turkey accepted Allied armistice terms. With Austria-

Hungary having sued for peace three days earlier, on November 3 fighting duly came to an end on the Italian Front in the Dolomite mountains.

Germany was now alone, with widespread civilian unrest and mutinies breaking out in the German Navy. On November 9, having lost the support of his government and people, Kaiser Wilhelm II abdicated and a republic was proclaimed in Germany. Armistice talks with the Allies were already ongoing, and at 11 a.m. on the eleventh day of the eleventh month the guns on the Western Front finally fell silent.

The war had seen the destruction of the old empires of Russia, Germany, Austria-Hungary, and Ottoman Turkey, and the emergence of new nation states in Central and Eastern Europe. But the new settlement, largely imposed by the Western Allies, did not put an end to the national and ethnic antagonisms that had always bedeviled Europe. Indeed, it was the failure to achieve a proper, lasting peace in 1918–19 that, along with a series of devastating economic crises in the 1920s and 1930s, created the conditions for a second, even more destructive global conflict just twenty years later.

BELOW
American troops are addressed by General "Jack" Pershing, commander of the US Army in France, in March 1919. Just three months later, a peace treaty between Germany and the Allies would be signed.

THE VERSAILLES TREATY

The peace treaty between Germany and the victorious Allies was signed at Versailles on June 28, 1919. The main terms of the treaty were confirmation of the loss of Germany's overseas colonies, the return of Alsace and Lorraine to France, the cessation of parts of Eastern Germany to Poland, the demilitarization of the Rhineland, and severe restrictions placed on the size and type of Germany's future armed forces. The German delegation signed the treaty under protest, particularly irked by a subsidiary clause that stated Germany must accept responsibility for starting the war. Unpopular throughout Germany, the seeming injustice of the Versailles Treaty was exploited by far-right parties and effectively repudiated by Adolf Hitler when the Nazis came to power in 1933.

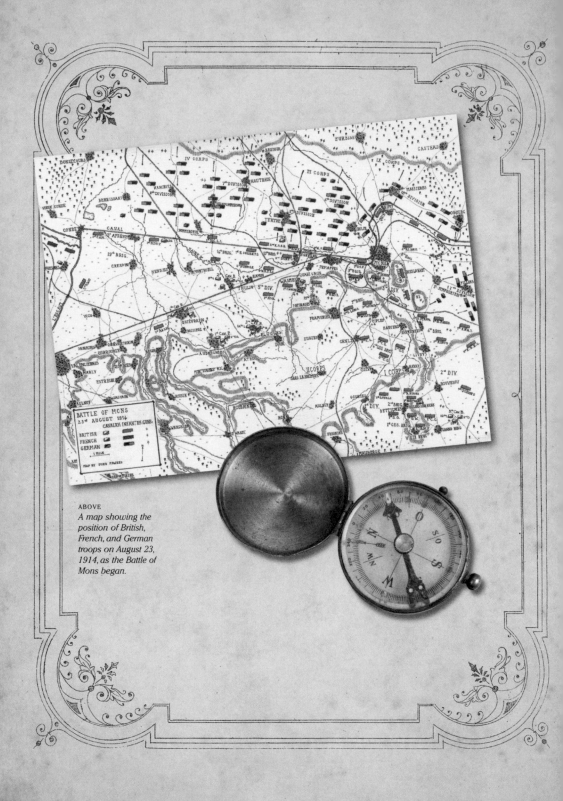

A map showing the position of British, French, and German troops on August 23, 1914, as the Battle of Mons began.

Robert DIGBY & Claire DESSENNE

Robert R. Digby

BRITISH

Born: 1885

Rank & regiment:
Private in the 1st Battalion,
Hampshire Regiment

Claire Dessenne

FRENCH

Born: 1897

Commandement supérieur de l'Armée.   Grand Quartier de l'Armée, le 30 Mars 1916.

ORDONNANCE.

1. Des personnes faisant partie des armées ennemies ont encore été arrêtées en France occupée par nos troupes, des indigènes leur ayant donné l'hospitalité.

Par conséquent, j'ordonne :

Les personnes qui, pendant la guerre, faisaient partie d'une armée ennemie ou étaient à sa suite et qui, actuellement, se trouvent en territoire occupé par les troupes allemandes, sont engagées à se présenter à une troupe ou Commandanture allemande jusqu'au 30 avril 1916, au plus tard.

Quiconque se présentera en temps voulu, restera impuni et sera traité comme prisonnier de guerre.

Tous ceux arrêtés après le 30 avril 1916, seront punis de la peine de mort ou dans un cas moins grave, de réclusion.

Chacun ayant nourri, logé ou aidé un soldat ennemi, ainsi que ceux s'étant dispensés de rapporter, sans retard, l'existence d'un individu de ce genre à l'autorité militaire la plus proche, seront punis de réclusion (5 ans au moins), plus d'une amende pouvant atteindre 10.000 Marks, en vertu de l'ordonnance du Armée-Oberkommando du 1er Octobre 1915. Dans un cas moins grave la punition peut aller jusqu'à 2 ans de prison ; en outre, on pourra infliger une amende s'élevant jusqu'à 3.000 Marks ou n'appliquer qu'une seule de ces peines.

Cette ordonnance ne comprend pas les soldats français ayant terminé leur service militaire et étant appelés, lors de la mobilisation :

   1. AU SERVICE DE REQUISITION DES CHEVAUX ET VOITURES ;
   2. AU SERVICE DE GARDE DES VOIES DE COMMUNICATION :
   3. AUX SERVICES AUXILIAIRES (ETABLISSEMENT DE CANTONNEMENTS, COMPAGNIES D'OUVRIERS, ETC.)
à la condition qu'ils n'ont porté, pendant ce service, ni armes, ni habit militaire — sauf les postes et patrouilles du service de garde des voies de communication — et qu'ils ont été régulièrement renvoyés après avoir fini leur tâche.

II. Toutes les armes blanches, à feu, tranchantes ou pointues (y compris les pièces héréditaires, rouillées et hors de service, les fusils de chasse et toute arme faisant partie d'une collection ou servant d'ornement mural ou d'objet d'art) ainsi que les cartouches de tout genre, les explosifs et obus, doivent être remis à l'autorité militaire allemande, jusqu'au 30 avril 1916 au plus tard.

Restera impuni chacun qui remettra ses armes en temps voulu.

Si des armes ou des cartouches seront trouvées après le 30 avril 1916, le détenteur ainsi que le propriétaire devront subir la peine de mort. Dans un cas moins grave, il seront frappés d'emprisonnement (réclusion jusqu'à 15 ans ou prison jusqu'à 5 ans). En outre,, on pourra infliger une amende s'élevant jusqu'à 15.000 Marks ou n'appliquer qu'une seule de ces peines.

III. Les maires ou administrateurs des communes :
   Où on arrêtera un soldat ennemi après le 30 avril 1916,
   Où un soldat ennemi s'est caché, et
   Où on trouvera des armes ou des cartouches après la date indiquée, seront frappés d'emprisonnement (réclusion jusqu'à 15 ans ou prison jusqu'à 5 ans). En outre, on pourra infliger une amende s'élevant jusqu'à 15.000 Marks ou n'appliquer qu'une seule de ces peines.

Toute commune dont la population est susceptible d'avoir sa part de responsabilité des infractions indiquées, devra s'attendre à une amende élevée.

Le Général Commandant en Chef,
Général der Infanterie.
v. BELOW.

According to this April 1916 notice posted in Villeret's town hall, all British soldiers who surrendered before April 30 would be held as prisoners of war, but after that any found would be shot.

"THEY FELL FOR ONE ANOTHER: BOOM! JUST LIKE THAT!" SAID CLAIRE'S GRANDMOTHER. THERE WAS NOTHING ANYONE COULD DO TO SEPARATE THEM—UNTIL THEY ENDURED THE ULTIMATE BETRAYAL.

Villeret in northeastern France is an isolated little hamlet surrounded by dense woods and rolling fields of wheat, rye and hay, where poppies bloom in summer. In 1914 most residents lived off the land and tended livestock, although some of the men worked in a nearby phosphate mine, doing tough work they would later learn had damaged their lungs. When war came, the able-bodied went off to fight, leaving their mothers, wives, and daughters to tend the home fires.

One such household was run by feisty matriarch Marie Coulette Dessenne, who lived in the Rue d'en Bas with her son, Florency, her daughter-in-law, Eugénie, and her granddaughter, Claire. Her other son, Hugo, Claire's father, had gone to fight. German troops moved in to occupy the area and Marie Coulette complied grudgingly with the new regulations requiring them to declare all their livestock and crops, and give a proportion to feed the invaders. Household items—pots, pans, cutlery—were requisitioned, and if the Germans saw any possession they desired during routine searches they simply helped themselves.

BELOW
Everyone knew everyone else in Villeret, where extended families lived side by side, but that didn't mean they always got along.

> ...*Claire was a great beauty ... with her grandmother's lively character.*

Seventeen-year-old Claire was a great beauty, with long, chestnut hair and her grandmother's lively character. She hated the way the German soldiers' eyes followed her in the road, and resented the enforced restrictions on their movements in and out of the area because she yearned for excitement and romance. A few local boys had tried to woo her, but with no success. And then one night in September 1914, there was a knock on their door. She opened it to see a tall, blonde, blue-eyed, very handsome twenty-nine-year-old Englishman, who asked in halting French if they could spare any food. Her heart was lost in an instant.

"Wholesale Rout and Slaughter"

Robert Digby never wanted to join the army. His father had been a career officer, but Robert tried different jobs, working for a time as a barman in a Parisian café where he learned to speak passable French, then setting himself up as a pig farmer in his home town of Totton in Hampshire. The pig farm collapsed and in 1913 both Robert and his brother Thomas volunteered for the Royal Hampshire Regiment, then the following year were shipped across the Channel with the British Expeditionary Force (BEF). On August 22, they were taken to the Franco-Belgian border near Mons, where the plan was that they should make a stand on the Mons-Condé Canal and prevent the advancing German army from encircling the Allies. The problem was that there were 80,000 of them and 160,000 Germans.

Battle began on the morning of August 23 and at first British riflemen managed to hold back the enemy, inflicting heavy losses, but by afternoon it became clear that their position was untenable. At 3 p.m. the order was given to begin the retreat, but the Germans pursued them, forcing them to fight a hasty rearguard action. One private, Frank Pattenden, wrote that "it was nearly wholesale rout and slaughter." The British fought bravely and managed to hold up the German 1st Army for 48 hours, but at great cost: of the 80,000 men in the BEF, 20,000 were killed, wounded, captured, or simply missing. And among the missing was Robert Digby.

During the retreat, his unit was engaged in a skirmish in the village of Villers-Outréaux in which he was wounded in the arm. He stopped to get treatment at a field station and then returned to

OPPOSITE
"The Bowmen of Mons," an illustration of the ghostly archers printed in the London Illustrated News, *1915. The rumors of angels helping the British troops inspired countless short stories, paintings, and songs, but researchers failed to find any convincing first-hand reports.*

THE ANGELS
OF MONS

The Battle of Mons was the first
battle of the Great War, and
although British troops were
vastly outnumbered and ultimately
overwhelmed, it seemed miraculous
that they managed to hold back
German troops for as long as they
did. On September 29, 1914,
Welsh author Arthur Machen wrote
a short story in which shimmering
ghosts of English bowmen killed at
Agincourt 500 years earlier came
to help the English army at Mons.
The Evening News ran the story
as fact rather than fiction and soon
anecdotes began to circulate of
men who claimed to have seen
these supernatural bowmen as
well as dozens of angels, helping
to delay the German forces. Many
soldiers were utterly convinced
they had seen these apparitions,
and the stories were tacitly
encouraged by British military
intelligence. What better morale-
booster could there be for their
troops than the notion that the
angels were on their side?

where his unit had been, only to find that his comrades were either dead or had retreated as the Germans had advanced, leaving him on the wrong side of the lines. He tramped cross-country through fields and woods, trying to find a safe route across to British lines, and along the way met other stragglers in the same position. Seven of them teamed up, reckoning they had a better chance together than alone. They scavenged what food they could find but were starving and gaunt when in mid-September they arrived in Villeret and Robert risked knocking on the door of the Dessenne family.

The Illicit Guests

When Marie Coulette saw the state the Englishmen were in, she invited them to sleep in her hayloft, although she was risking arrest for harboring Allied soldiers. It was only a matter of time before her neighbors found out and word spread around the village.

The villagers could have handed the fugitives over to the German occupiers to keep themselves out of trouble, but the Germans were hated and Robert Digby in particular was very charming, so they decided the village would harbor them. They would stay in attics and work the fields, learning the region's patois and passing themselves off as locals until they could find a way to slip across German lines and rejoin their army. Villagers were proud to have

BELOW
A view of the village of Villeret in 1914; by the war's end, all its buildings, including the church, had been destroyed.

taken a stance against the occupation and soon the seven men became known as "our Englishmen."

Robert was given false papers in the name of Robert Boitelle and lodged in the attic of local woman Susanne Boitelle. Robert had aristocratic bearing, sublime manners, and was so much liked by the local women that when Marie-Thérèse Dessenne, Claire's aunt, gave birth to her

> *When challenged, Claire admitted the truth to her mother——that they were very much in love.*

fourth child in spring 1915, she named him Robert in honor of the English guest. But not long afterward, It was observed that Robert and young Claire were spending a suspicious amount of time alone together, slipping off for long walks or up to her family's hayloft. When challenged, Claire admitted the truth to her mother—that they were very much in love.

Although she liked Robert, Claire's mother disapproved of the relationship. Who would want her daughter linked to a fugitive with an uncertain future? She asked Claire's cousins Emile and Julie to spy on them, but Claire caught Emile spying and persuaded him to come to their side, acting as lookout to warn them when others were coming. There was nothing that could be done—especially when it became obvious to all that Claire was carrying Robert's child.

Food was increasingly scarce by the autumn of 1915. All livestock, milk, and eggs were requisitioned for the German army, and white bread was only ever seen on German tables. After the birth of Claire and Robert's baby on November 14, 1915—a girl they called Hélène after his mother Ellen—villagers began to mutter about the extra mouths they had to feed. Three of the visitors had managed to escape back to British lines, but the four that remained showed no signs of leaving. Attitudes to them began to change, imperceptibly at first and then more obviously. Robert was so caught up with his baby daughter, whom he proudly paraded in his arms up and down the village streets, that he failed to pick up on the change of mood.

In spring 1916 the Germans put up signs saying that all British soldiers who surrendered before April 30, would be held as prisoners of war; after that would they be shot and any French citizens who had helped them would be fined and imprisoned. It would only take one person in the village to betray them, and that's exactly what happened on May 15, 1916.

In the early hours of the 16th, the hayloft where the four men were sleeping was raided by German troops; three were captured but Robert Digby managed to leap out of a window and escape into the woods. He hid there for five days, unable to get a message back to Claire because of all the German soldiers who'd been posted on sentry duty. The village's acting mayor Emile Marié guessed he must be in the woods and came to find him. He said that if Robert were to give himself up, the Germans had promised his life would be spared, but that if he stayed at large there would be dreadful reprisals against all who had helped him—including Claire and Hélène. There was no choice. A couple of days later, on May 22, Robert walked out of the woods and surrendered. He was tried by a German military court at Le Câtelet, accused of spying, and sentenced to death. Emile Marié's promise of amnesty had been untrue.

BELOW
The letter Robert wrote to Claire from his prison cell in Le Câtelet hours before his death, sending her a kiss and asking her to tell his daughter about him one day.

Câtelet
l'Aisne
May 30th 1916

Ma chérie Claire la lettre dernière de
ma vie Je suis condamné à mort
être fusillé à dix heures cinq
minutes au soir. Aurevoir et n'oublie
jamais Robert étant heureux et
content pour la France et pour
mon pays. Une baisée pour vous.
Donnez une pour ma fille et après
elle est grande. Disez la vérité de
son père qui a mort heureusement.
Envoyez vous la lettre déja écrire pour
ma mère. J'ai donné une lettre à
Monsieur le Pasteur pour chez moi
parceque les Allemands arreté les lettres
de mes camarades

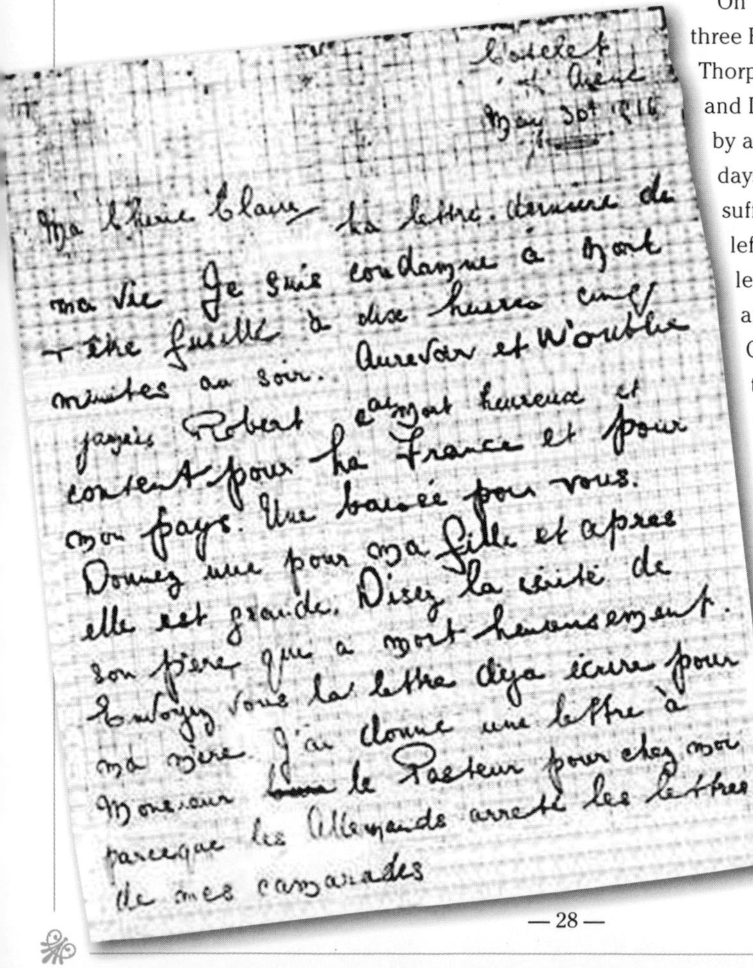

On May 27, 1916, the first three Englishmen—William Thorpe, Thomas Donohoe, and David Martin—were killed by a firing squad, and three days later Robert Digby suffered the same fate. He left behind a very stoical letter for his own mother, an apologetic letter for Claire's mother asking her to look after Claire and the child, and three letters for Claire herself: "Tell the child not to weep for me, for I have brought her into a world of such unhappiness . . . Embrace my baby girl and later, when she is grown, tell her the truth about her father, who has died contented."

LEFT
*Hélène and Claire in 1925.
Hélène, known to locals
as* "la tiote anglaise"
*(the little English girl),
had her father's stunning
blue eyes.*

The child grows up

Marie-Thérèse and Florency Dessenne were sentenced to ten years' hard labor and fined 10,000 marks for sheltering the Englishmen. Suzanne Boitelle got 23 months in a German prison. The Lelongs, the village bakers, and Achille Poëtte, the postman, were also imprisoned and an additional fine was imposed on the village as a whole. No one knew who had betrayed the Englishman but rumors and theories abounded. Had it been Léon Lelong, whose daughter had been in love with Robert? Achille Poëtte, who had been in love with Claire? Victor Marié, a local spy? Why had Mayor Émile Marié's son, who'd been arrested at the same time as the first three Englishmen, been released without charge after Robert's execution? No one knew for sure but there were a lot of bitter accusations behind closed doors. Marie Coulette concentrated on looking after Marie-Thérèse and Florency's children, and Claire looked after baby Hélène, counting themselves lucky to have avoided punishment.

In that summer of 1916, Villeret became the location of dozens of makeshift field hospitals to accommodate the wounded from the Battle of the Somme, and in February 1917 the village was evacuated and the villagers were taken to a refugee camp in the Ardennes. Buildings were reduced to rubble and the wood where Robert Digby had hidden hacked down as the German army retreated, so as not to provide any succor for advancing British troops. When villagers returned in 1918, they were so horrified that many chose to move elsewhere rather than rebuild their properties from scratch. Those who had been imprisoned were released, now very thin and with their health impaired due to the harsh conditions.

ESPIONAGE BEHIND ENEMY LINES

Victor Marié was a smuggler and small-town crook who offered his services as a spy to the Allies in 1914. He reported back to the British about troop movements, ammunition depots, and the railway network in Occupied France, and created a network of around sixty spies that was known as *'Réseau Victor'* (Victor Network). They used homing pigeons to pass information across enemy lines; over 100,000 homing pigeons were used during World War One, and it

is estimated that they successfully delivered their messages in 95 percent of cases. In July 1916, Victor Marié was presented with a Distinguished Conduct Medal by General Haig, but at the end of that year the network he had created was uncovered by the Germans and there were mass arrests and executions—though not of Victor Marié. Suspicions grew that he had changed allegiance and betrayed his countrymen. He died in 1919 at the age of forty-three, and rumors in the village were that the cause of death was poisoning.

LEFT
Spy Victor Marié, who described Digby as "a true Englishman."

BELOW
Pigeons had accurate homing instincts and were almost impossible to shoot down, making them ideal for carrying messages.

After the war Claire got work in a textile factory near Villeret, and was awarded a bronze medal by the British government in gratitude for the "valuable service she had rendered" in protecting the men. She forwarded Robert's letter to his mother, explained that she had a granddaughter, and passed on Robert's request that she should acknowledge and help to support the child —but no word of reply ever came from the proud Ellen Digby. Perhaps she didn't want his name to be besmirched by the revelation that he had fathered a "bastard," and that's why she didn't acknowledge the girl who was known to Villeret residents as *"la tiote anglaise"* (the little English girl).

Ellen Digby died in 1929, and while going through her papers her son Thomas came across the letter that Robert had sent from his condemned cell the night before he died, along with the letter from Claire. He was furious that his mother had kept such a huge secret from him, and in the summer of 1930 he made the emotional journey to Villeret to meet his brother's daughter, who was now fourteen years of age and had bright blue eyes just like her father's. It was said they were "as alike as two drops of water." The family all went to the mayor's office where Thomas signed a document recognizing Hélène as his own daughter, and on her birth certificate the name Dessenne was scored out and replaced with the surname Digby.

It wasn't verified during their lifetimes who had betrayed Robert, but Hélène recounted that her mother always "had it in for" Emile Marié, the mayor, and that she "wanted him dead." In 2009, four years after Hélène's death, an archive was discovered in the Royal Museum of the Armed Forces in Brussels containing a statement from local spy Victor Marié which said that "Robert was denounced by the mayor of Villeret." It makes sense: in return for the lives of the fugitive Englishmen, his own son was spared.

In 1933, Hélène married a man called Hubert Cornaille from the neighboring village of Le Verguier. Shortly after, Claire married the foreman of the textile factory where she worked, but by all accounts it was a marriage of companionship and Robert remained the love of her life. She often went to place a blue hydrangea on his grave, in memory of those startlingly blue eyes she would never forget.

ABOVE
Proud Ellen Digby always refused to acknowledge the illegitimate grand-daughter who was named after her, despite her son's final wishes.

ABOVE
Ivor wrote regularly to his friend Marion Scott while he was in Bangour War Hospital.

RIGHT
Ivor's poem, "Spring, Rouen, May 1917," expresses his deep homesickness for England. It was published in October 1917 in the book Severn and Somme.

Ivor
GURNEY
&
Annie
DRUMMOND

Ivor Bertie Gurney	**Annie Nelson Drummond**
BRITISH	SCOTTISH
—	—
Born: August 28, 1890	*Born: November 9, 1887*
—	—
Rank & regiment: Private in the 2/5th Gloucestershire Regiment then gunner in the 184th Machine Gun Company	*War work: Voluntary Aid Detachment (VAD) nurse*

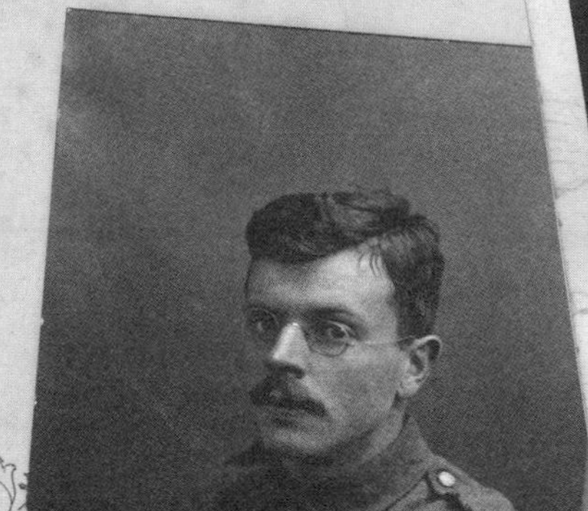

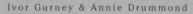

ABOVE
*Ivor at Christmas 1917 while
in the hospital in Seaton Delaval,
Northumberland, a place he called
a "freezing, ugly, uncomfortable Hell
of a Hole." He was worried by the
lack of letters from Annie.*

**IVOR AND ANNIE'S RELATIONSHIP WAS INTENSE AND PASSIONATE.
HE WROTE TO A FRIEND THAT HER "BEAUTIFUL SIMPLICITY" REMINDED
HIM OF "THE KIND OF FUNDAMENTAL SWEET FIRST THING ONE GETS
IN BACH, NOT TO BE DESCRIBED, ONLY TREASURED."**

I vor Gurney was the second of four surviving children of a
tailor. His mother Florence was a highly strung woman who
didn't enjoy motherhood so that, according to his sister
Winifred, life for the children was "something akin to a bed of
stinging nettles." Fortunately for Ivor he had a godfather, the
Reverend Alfred Cheesman, who recognized his musical and
literary abilities. He encouraged the boy to apply for a choral
scholarship at Gloucester Cathedral, which he achieved, as well
as giving him access to his library and introducing him to poetry.
Ivor began composing his own music at the age of fourteen and
in 1911 won a scholarship to the Royal College of Music in London.
It was there he met a half-American woman, Marion Scott, who was
to become one of the most significant figures in his life.

Marion was thirteen years older than Ivor, a published
poet and accomplished violinist with a wide circle
of contacts in the musical and literary worlds.
She had formed the Royal College of Music
Union, to enable former students to stay
in touch with each other, as well as the
Society of Women Musicians, and she
organized a program of concerts and
teas for both groups. Physically fragile,
she was immensely strong-willed and,
having befriended Ivor, she became
his champion for life. It is possible that
he was briefly infatuated with her, but
his feelings were soon confirmed in
his mind as those of close friendship,
while hers for him appear to have
deepened into love.

Ivor was a handsome, immensely
charming man, but he had long been
prone to manic episodes followed by
periods of severe depression. At college

BELOW
*Marion Scott wrote
articles on music for a
number of magazines
and helped to promote
female musicians. She
would prove to be Ivor's
greatest champion and
most loyal friend.*

he talked wildly of writing great operas and symphonies but was not able to produce them. His composition teacher, Sir Charles Villiers Stanford, said that Ivor may have been the most gifted pupil ever to pass through the college but that he was fundamentally "unteachable." In 1913, under the pressure of work, getting little sleep, and eating poorly, Ivor suffered a serious mental breakdown during which he considered suicide. He had to take time off college and return to his beloved Gloucestershire countryside to recuperate.

By July 1914 Ivor was well enough to return to college and when war was declared he tried to enlist immediately, only to be refused because of his poor eyesight. In February 1915 he was accepted by the 2/5th Gloucestershires, and set off for basic training. He wrote to a friend, "It is indeed a better way to die; with these men, in such a cause; than the end which seemed near to me and was so desirable only just over two years ago." The physical exertion of military training combined with a balanced diet and regular hours made him happier than he had felt for some time, and he set off for the Front determined to prove himself.

> *"It is indeed a better way to die; with these men, in such a cause ..."*

Into Battle

In the trenches of France, Ivor began writing poetry, describing the horrors of war and contrasting it with the beauty of his native Gloucester. Marion Scott was his most regular correspondent, and he began sending poems for her critical appraisal. She kept him supplied with notebooks and manuscript paper for his compositions, as well as lemonade crystals, tobacco, and insect repellent. He wrote, "Your letters are as stars in the night, or blinks of sunlight—promises of blue." Physically, Ivor was brave—"in hand to hand fighting I'd be dangerous to tackle," he wrote to Marion—and he proved to be a crack shot. He was wounded in the upper arm in April 1917 and spent a month in hospital in Rouen before returning to the Front. On July 15, he was told he was to be transferred to the 184th Machine Gun Company, who were headed for Ypres, and just 30 minutes after this news he heard from Marion that Sidgwick & Jackson wanted to publish his collected war poems. They would come out that autumn under the title *Severn and Somme*.

Between June and November 1917, Ypres was the site of the bitterly fought Battle of Passchendaele and, as soon as he arrived,

Ivor was aware of the heightened danger. A German pilot was shot down and the body landed "not 30 yards" from him. He was hit twice by shrapnel that dented his helmet. Then on September 17, in St-Julien, he was caught in a German mustard-gas attack that ended his war career. Although he later wrote to Marion that "Being gassed (mildly) with the new gas is no worse than catarrh or a bad cold," his health was seriously affected and he was shipped back to the UK. From a list of hospitals, he chose to be sent to Bangour in Edinburgh and arrived there on September 23, too ill to walk to his bed in Ward 24.

After sixteen months at the Front, Ivor enjoyed "the sheets white and smooth" as well as the plentiful supply of food from a farm on site. Before long he was able to get out of bed and play the piano, and soon an attractive, young Scottish Voluntary Aid nurse named Annie Drummond caught his attention.

Annie had been born in Armadale, West Lothian, the eldest of five children. Her mother was a milliner and her father a coal miner, so with both parents working it became her responsibility to look after her four younger brothers. She also found time to take piano lessons and had a particular love of flowers, birds, and the outdoors. Once her brothers were old enough to fend for

ABOVE
Ivor with members of the 2/5th Gloucester Battalion, training in June/July 1915. The regimented army life suited him and he set off for the Front full of enthusiasm for the fight ahead.

ABOVE
*Ivor in hospital in Rouen,
where he spent a month
recovering from a
gunshot wound to the
upper arm, received on
Good Friday, 1917.*

themselves, she began to study nursing and when
war broke out she switched to the Scottish Red
Cross to complete her studies, before volunteering
to work at the Edinburgh War Hospital at Bangour.
It was only nine miles from her home, but she lived
at the hospital because the hours were so long.
It was a well-run institution, founded in June 1915
in the premises of an asylum for the mentally insane.
Top medical specialists came to work there and it
was quickly at the forefront of orthopaedic and
disease treatment in the UK, as well as having
plenty of experience of treating gas attacks. Ivor
was in good hands.

At first he was too weak to do much. Even
drying dishes after a meal tired him, but he began having long
conversations with Annie about music, nature, and poetry. She was
just a month short of her thirtieth birthday and in her prime. Ivor
described her in a letter to a friend as having "a pretty figure, pretty
hair, fine eyes, pretty hands and arms and walk. A charming voice,
pretty ears, a resolute little mouth." At first she appeared to have
"a mask on her face more impenetrable than any other woman
I have seen," but soon this melted and she told Ivor that she had
never met anyone as talented and romantic as he, and that being

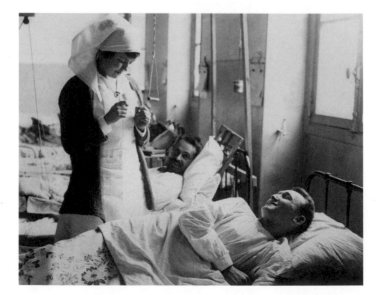

RIGHT
*Nurses were forbidden
from forming romantic
liaisons with patients, but
many ignored the rules.*

with him lifted her thoughts out of the daily routine.
She enjoyed listening to him playing his compositions
and reading his poems, and all in all thought he was
quite the most interesting man she had ever met.

> "I forgot my body walking with her."

Once Ivor was well enough, they began to take
walks in the surrounding countryside during her time
off, and he was so smitten that he forgot about the unpleasant
digestive and respiratory symptoms he was still suffering from
the gas attack. "I forgot my body walking with her," he wrote to
a friend. "A thing that has not happened since."

All too soon, on November 17, Ivor was transferred to a hospital
in Northumberland, but he wrote regularly to Annie and, although
she was slower in responding than he would have liked, he
dedicated his new collection of poems "to Puck," one of his pet
names for her. Throughout this time, Ivor was careful not to let
Marion Scott, who was acting as his literary agent and manager,
get wind of the affair. He must have known about
Marion's feelings for him and didn't want to
make her jealous and risk losing her goodwill.

A Major Breakdown

In early January 1918 Ivor was able to travel to
Edinburgh for a weekend with Annie. They had
"A glorious but bitterly cold Sunday evening.
A snowy but intimate Monday evening," and
afterward he wrote to a friend that he wanted
to settle down with Annie and make "a solid
rock foundation for me to build on—a home
and a tower of light." He asked his sister to
have his cap badge dipped in gold and
turned into a brooch for Annie, and it seems
that although he hadn't given her a ring,
he considered himself engaged to her and
began asking her to set a date for their
marriage. He wrote a poem for her—
"My heart makes song on lonely roads/
To comfort me while you're away"—and
said her letters to him made him feel as
if she were there, "whispering most
comforting things."

BELOW
*A note from the
Edinburgh War Hospital
requesting Ivor Gurney's
medical records. He chose
to be treated so far from
home partly because he
didn't want visitors.*

GAS ATTACKS

The first gas attack of the war was launched by the French, who in August 1914 threw tear-gas grenades to hinder a German advance, but in April 1915 at Ypres, the Germans used chlorine gas delivered from pressurized cylinders, causing French troops to flee in terror. In September 1915, the British released chlorine at Loos, but the wind changed direction, making it drift back over their own lines. Phosgene gas was the next used, and this was particularly terrifying as it was hard to detect and didn't cause symptoms for 48 hours, by which time little could be done to counteract the effects on the body. Mustard gas was used by the Germans in September 1917, and this caused suppurating yellow blisters to the sufferer that affected their eyes, skin, respiratory, digestive, and other body systems. It is thought that around 1.25 million men were injured by gas attacks during the war and, while fewer than 10 percent died of it at the time, they suffered from prolonged illnesses that incapacitated them in later life.

Ivor hoped to see Annie again in February but had to postpone the trip after losing a ten-pound note as he didn't have any more money for the train fare. He was struck down again with stomach trouble caused by the gas attack and while recovering in hospital he received a bombshell: a letter from Annie breaking off their engagement. She never explained this action, but perhaps Ivor's possessiveness was becoming obsessive to the point that it alarmed her. He seems to have been in a manic phase and writing odd things to friends, so maybe she caught a glimpse of his madness and was afraid of what she saw. Whatever the reason, she ended the relationship, and this was the final straw that plummeted him into a huge and very severe mental breakdown in which he heard voices and displayed psychotic behavior.

In a letter to Marion Scott in April, Ivor told her of an encounter he claimed to have had with the spirit of Beethoven, and this worried her enough to seek help for him. He was moved from one hospital to

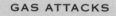

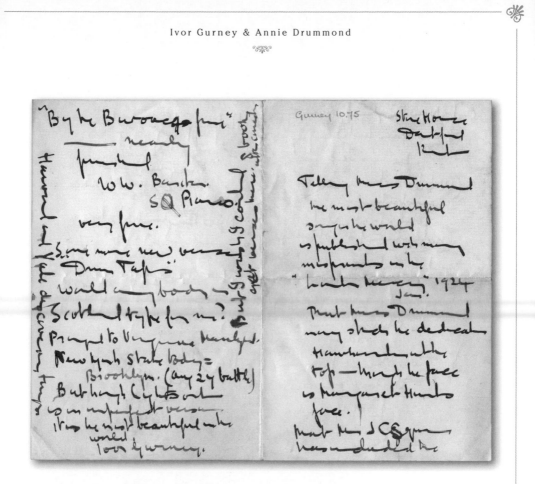

another before ending up at Kings Weston near Bristol, a place that dealt with cases of shellshock. Then, on October 4, he was discharged from the army suffering from "Manic Depressive Psychosis," which according to his discharge papers was "aggravated by but not due to service."

Throughout 1918, Ivor kept writing to Annie without getting a reply. He sent presents, including a new book of his poetry entitled *Poems of To-Day*, with the inscription, "To Nurse Drummond with thanks for joy and best wishes for all things to come." Still there was no reply. Eventually, in desperation, he told Marion about Annie and begged her to write on his behalf. Marion was upset to hear he had been engaged, and described Annie in a letter to a friend as "the lively VAD who played fast and loose with Ivor till she drove him to desperation … who thereafter refused to have any communication with him." In her view, Annie broke off the engagement when she found out the celebrated war poet was "insane and poor." Another friend wrote, "As for the Drummond girl, I don't suppose she ever arrived at an understanding of what she had done."

ABOVE
A letter Ivor wrote to Annie in October/ November 1924, by which time he was living in a Gloucestershire mental hospital.

OPPOSITE
Early gas masks worn by men in the trenches in 1915 offered insufficient protection. Box respirators, a two-piece design comprising a mouthpiece connected to a box filter which neutralized the harmful gases, were first issued to British troops in April 1916 in time for the Battle of the Somme.

Ivor's mental health continued to be delicate after the war
and in September 1922 his family had him committed to Barnwood
House mental hospital in Gloucester, where he lived until his death
from tuberculosis at the age of forty-seven. In 1924 he tried once
more to contact Annie, prevailing on Marion to write to her
mother, but the reply came that Annie had emigrated to the US in
1921 and was living with her husband in Wellesley, Massachusetts.

Life had not been kind to Ivor. Although his poems and music
received universal acclaim, his life in the asylum was torture for
a man who loved open countryside and the society of his friends.
Life was not kind to Annie either. Soon after she arrived in Wellesley
with her Scottish husband, Sgt. James McKay, another patient she

Life had not been kind to Ivor. Although his poems and music received universal acclaim, his life in the asylum was torture.

had cared for at Bangour Hospital, there was a fire in their house from which Annie managed to save only a few photographs, her nursing certificates, and the book of poems Ivor had sent her in 1918. In 1931 their seven-year-old son John was killed by a runaway truck while playing in front of their home. And in the 1950s, Annie's mental health deteriorated to the extent that she had to spend the last eight years of her life in hospital.

Annie and Ivor's love had been sweet and true during the winter of 1917–18, and if she decided not to commit herself to a man with mental health problems whom she had only known for six months, one who couldn't visit her because he'd lost his last ten-pound note, then who can blame her? But it seems Annie never forgot her lively, talented fiancé. After her death, her daughter Peggy Ann looked through the old leather suitcase in which she kept all her most precious belongings and found the score of a song cycle, "Western Playland," that Ivor had dedicated to Annie, along with the inscribed book of poems she had saved from the fire.

WAR POETS

Rupert Brooke was known as the first of the war poets but in fact his famously patriotic works, such as "The Soldier" ("If I should die, think only this of me;/That there's some corner of a foreign field/That is forever England."), were written without him seeing any action. He died in April 1915 of an infected mosquito bite while on his way to Gallipoli. The poets who described the horrors of the trenches and were fiercely critical of the war included Wilfred Owen (who wrote "Anthem for Doomed Youth," with the opening line, "What passing bells for these who die as cattle?"); Siegfried Sassoon ("The rank stench of those bodies haunts me still"); Herbert Read, who wrote about a deserter in "The Execution of Cornelius Vane"; and Ivor Gurney (in "The Silent One" he wrote of a soldier "Who died on the wires, and hung there, one of two"). These poets shared a skepticism about religion. If God existed, they asked, why did he allow men to suffer so?

LEFT
Rupert Brooke, known as the first of the war poets, did not live to witness the war, after dying on his way to Gallipoli.

RIGHT
A German poster encouraging men to enlist: "Your Fatherland is in Danger," it reads.

BELOW
Max had already won some acclaim as an artist before the war began.

Max ERNST & Luise STRAUS-ERNST

Married: October 7, 1918

Max Ernst

GERMAN

Born: April 2, 1891

Rank & regiment:
Lieutenant, 36th Regiment,
Rhineland Field Artillery

Luise Straus

GERMAN

Born: December 2, 1893

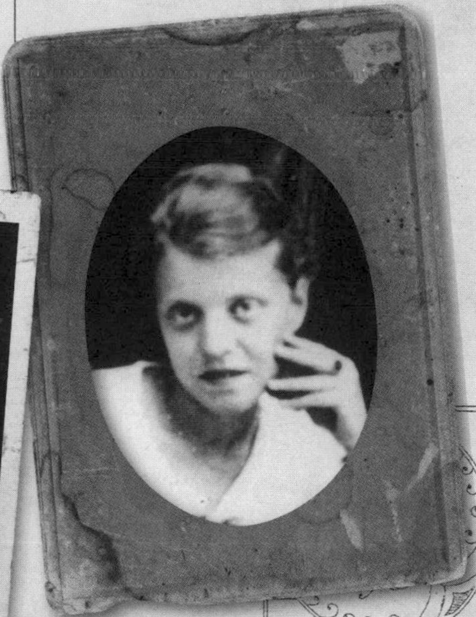

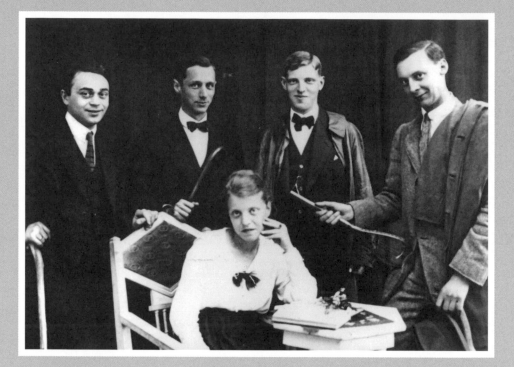

ABOVE

*Members of the Dadaist Society in Cologne in 1919: From left
to right, Hans Hansen, Max Ernst, Luise Straus, her brother
Richard, and Alfred Grünewald. "To us Dada was above all a
moral reaction … A horrible futile war had robbed us of five
years of our existence," they wrote in the review* Der Ventilator.

LUISE'S FAMILY WANTED HER TO MARRY A WEALTHY JEWISH MAN BUT INSTEAD, JUST BEFORE THE WAR BEGAN, SHE FELL IN LOVE WITH MAX, A HANDSOME, FREE-SPIRITED ARTIST WHO HAD BEEN RAISED A CATHOLIC.

L uise was the daughter of a Cologne hat maker and she grew up in a liberal, middle-class Jewish family. After school she studied art history at the University of Bonn and it was there, early in 1913, that she met Max, who was studying an eclectic range of subjects, including philosophy, literature, psychology, and psychiatry as well as art history. For about a year they were just casual acquaintances until one day Max sat next to Luise in the life-drawing class, a mandatory part of the art history course. Looking over her shoulder, he noticed she was struggling to complete her drawing so he surreptitiously took her pad and completed the figure for her. She already knew him as an artist whose work had appeared in a number of group exhibitions. His father Philipp was an amateur painter, and since 1909 Max had been producing his own sketches and portraits to some acclaim in avant-garde circles. He was influenced by Pablo Picasso, whose work he had seen at a 1912 exhibition in Cologne, and was also intrigued by the art produced by the mentally ill, sometimes visiting asylums to watch inmates paint.

Luise let Max walk her back to her dormitory that day and agreed to go out with him the following Sunday for a stroll along the Rhine. These strolls became a weekly event, and she often sat watching while he sketched on the riverbank. He assured her that he would never try to take her "by storm" but waited patiently for nine months, with chaste embraces his only reward, until

BELOW
A bridge over the Rhine in Bonn, c. 1918. A promenade ran along the banks of the river, where Max and Luise went strolling on Sundays.

Bonn a. Rh. - Rheinbrücke

she became sure of her feelings for him. One day he took her
upriver to a point where a jetty caused the water to swirl and flow
upstream and, as they held each other close, she knew she had
fallen in love with him. Her parents wanted her to marry a man
named Otto Keller, son of a prominent Jewish family in Cologne.
With Otto, she would have financial security, and she even
suggested to Max that perhaps she could marry one man and still
love another. She recorded his reply in her diary: "He said that I was
far too intelligent and vivacious to be buried in the mediocrity of
that way of life."

Both watched with mounting horror the Kaiser's militaristic
posturing and then the chain of events in summer 1914 that led
to Germany's declarations of war on Russia and France, and the
ultimatum to Belgium that brought Britain into the conflict. Max
enlisted straightaway; as a fit young man, he had no choice in the
matter. Just at the point when they declared their love for each
other, Max and Luise were torn apart, and neither had any idea
how long that separation would last—or, indeed, if they would
ever be reunited.

RIGHT
*Some think the Big
Bertha, a 16½ inch
howitzer, got its name
from Bertha Krupp,
heiress to the armaments
firm that built it.*

The War Years

In his regiment, Max was trained to fire the huge field guns
that were used to bombard enemy trenches before an attack
over no-man's-land. Between 1914 and 1916 he was moved
around to postings on the Rivers Meuse and Marne on the
Western Front, although it is not clear whether he took
part in the Battle of the Marne in September 1914 when
the Allies managed to halt the German offensive. Any vague
patriotism Max might have felt at the war's beginning was
soon destroyed by the senseless death, random brutality,
and horrific mutilation he witnessed in the trenches. Although
he spent some time charting maps, an activity that gave him
access to paints and allowed him to carry on with his art,
he soon became very depressed.

Every day Max wrote to Luise about the horrors he was
witnessing and she wrote back trying to raise his spirits, but the
letters were slow to arrive and heavily censored. Occasionally
he got a furlough and could travel to Cologne, where she was
still living with her parents. The time they spent together was
precious and passionate, sealing their feelings for each other and
providing Max with a yearned-for respite from the fighting. After
one visit in 1916, Luise missed her monthly period and, in a panic,
told her parents that she might be pregnant. They were furious,
her mother warning her that Max was a fly-by-night artist who
would probably never be seen again. How could she let this
happen? They would never be able to show their faces in Cologne
for shame. On the contrary, when he received the news in a letter
from Luise, Max applied for special leave and came home wearing
the full formal uniform and spiked Pickelhaube helmet in which
soldiers got married. He told Luise's parents that he was very much
in love with their daughter and there was no question but that he
would stand by her. In any event, the pregnancy turned out to be
a false alarm, but Luise and Max decided anyway that they wanted
to get married after the war was over.

The fighting dragged on, and Max was there for much of the
long and bloody Battle of Verdun between February and December
1916, during which German troops took Fort Douaumont from the
French, only to lose it again. Estimates of the number of casualties
vary, but it's thought that at least 377,000 Frenchmen and 337,000
Germans were killed. The whole area was turned to thick, viscous

> *"What a bloodbath, what horrid images, what a slaughter. ... Hell cannot be this dreadful."*

mud filled with fragments of human remains. Men drowned in huge, slippery shell holes from which they were unable to climb out, and the ghostly shadows of shattered trees stood out against the sky. A French soldier, Albert Joubaire, wrote, "What a bloodbath, what horrid images, what a slaughter. ... Hell cannot be this dreadful." All who were there shared his view.

From November 1916 to May 1917 Max was on the Eastern Front fighting the Russians through the depths of the long, bitterly cold winter, then by June 1917 was back near the Belgian border, where he was exposed to poison gas during a British attack. He was injured twice, though not in battle. On the first occasion a horse kicked him in the head while his men were trying to shoe it; on the second, he was hit by recoil while inspecting an artillery piece and his face swelled up badly. His fellow soldiers nicknamed him, "the man with the iron head."

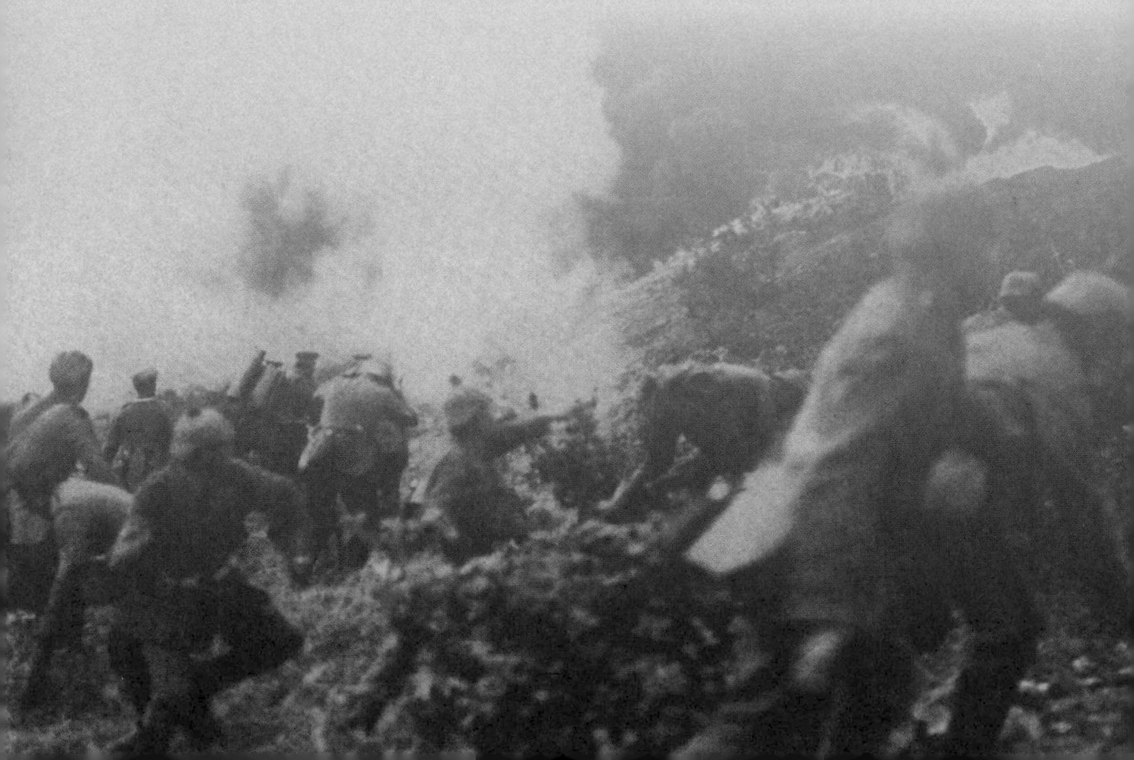

In September 1917 he was transferred to the 36th Regiment of Field Artillery, which at the time was being held in reserve. At last away from the front line, Ernst was promoted to the rank of lieutenant by his commander, a commission he tried but was not allowed to

BELOW
German troops attack on March 15, 1916, during the Battle of Verdun. It was the longest single battle of the war, lasting from February 21 to December 18, and saw the deaths of three quarters of a million French and German soldiers.

refuse. Instead, he showed his disgust for the war in another way. Several weeks before the Armistice, in August or September 1918, he marched his company of soldiers away from the Front and across France and Belgium to the other side of the Rhine, then told them they were dismissed and could all go home. Far from being chastised for this act of desertion, after the war he was awarded an Iron Cross for gallantry, an honor which this time he successfully turned down. All he wanted was to get back to his painting and to marry Luise, who had waited patiently for him right through the four years he had been away.

Both families were bitterly opposed to the marriage: Max's parents were prominent Catholics, and Luise's were devout Jews who doubted his ability to keep their daughter in the style to which she was accustomed. The only family members to attend their civil marriage ceremony on October 7, 1918, were Max's brother and sister. Both sets of parents stayed away. The newlyweds rented an apartment on the top floor of a townhouse on Kaiser-Wilhelm-Ring in Cologne, but money was short because their parents refused to help support them and work was thin on the ground for artists and art historians in the post-war period. Max was prone

FOOD SHORTAGES IN GERMANY

Britain imposed a naval blockade on Germany at the start of the war, meaning they couldn't import certain essential products, such as crop fertilizers, cotton, and rubber. On top of that, most able-bodied men were sent to the Front, leaving few behind to tend the farms and causing a reduction in available food rations. Troops were given priority when it came to food supplies, and soon the civilian population was having to make do with rationed Kriegsbrot (war bread), made from potatoes combined with a little wheat and rye flour, and margarine made from vegetable oil in place of butter. In the winter of 1916–17 a severe frost killed the potato harvest, so turnips became a major source of nutrition. By 1918, food shortages were affecting the troops as well. Meat rations had been reduced to 12 percent of their pre-war level and finely ground sawdust was used in bread in place of flour. Hundreds of thousands of German civilians died from malnutrition and soldiers got home from the Front to find their wives and children seriously thin and undernourished.

LEFT
A German ration card in 1915. Stamps were torn off in exchange for loaves of bread.

DESERTION

In the early years of the war, most soldiers remained committed to the fight, but cracks began to appear in the French Army in May and June 1917 when thousands of troops mutinied, refusing to move forward to the front lines. Of these, 3,335 soldiers were court-martialed and 449 were condemned to death, but fewer than a tenth of these were actually executed. During the war, 3,080 British soldiers were sentenced to death, most of them for desertion, but only 307 were shot while the rest were shipped off to the colonies. It's now believed that many deserters were suffering from shellshock and in some countries they have since been posthumously pardoned. In 1916, thousands of Czechs deserted; during 1917 tens of thousands of Russians ran off; then in December 1917, 300,000 Turkish soldiers left their lines. By the end of August 1918, with acute food shortages and plummeting morale, desertion from the German Army was becoming common and Max was not alone in heading home several weeks before the Armistice.

RIGHT
German deserters cross the frozen River Meuse into Holland searching for refuge from the fighting.

to dark moods and periods of introspection or short temper, with memories of the war haunting his sleeping and waking hours. He'd had a tough war by anyone's standards and it changed him irrevocably. He later wrote in his autobiography, "On the first of August 1914 M.[ax] E.[rnst] died. He was resurrected on the eleventh of November 1918." But Max and Luise were happy to be together at last and both were overjoyed in June 1920 when she gave birth to a son, whom they named Ulrich, but whom everyone would call Jimmy.

Art over Love

The Dadaist movement had begun in Zurich in 1916 as an intellectual protest against the war and what its founders saw as the petty rules of bourgeois society, but in Germany in 1919 it became a style of art characterized by nihilist images created using techniques such as collage

Des déserteurs allemands passent la Meuse glacée pour se réfugier en Hollande

and montage. Encouraged by his friend Hans (better known as
Jean) Arp, Max began to create bizarre collages full of dreamlike
images of violence and religious and sexual imagery. Along with
a number of colleagues he founded a Cologne branch of the
Dadaist movement and Luise became its secretary. Soon their
apartment was overrun by visiting artists, poets, and art critics,
who slept wherever they could find a space. Luise became the
hostess whose job it was to find food for these peripatetic house
guests; to make ends meet she took odd jobs, selling hosiery at
the Tietz department store, or typing in offices. A nanny called
Maja was hired to look after their little boy, while Max and Jean
organized Cologne's first Dada exhibition, a strange event set in
a pub, which was entered through a men's urinal, and at which
obscene poetry was read aloud by a woman wearing a Communion
dress. The provocative, anti-religious imagery of the exhibits
managed to upset both Max's and Luise's parents even more than
ever. Undeterred, Luise devoted all her efforts to supporting Max
in his endeavors, sublimating her own life to his and pandering to
his volatile mood swings.

ABOVE
*The opening of the
exhibition "Dada Max
Ernst" at the Au Sans
Pareil gallery in Paris
on May 2, 1921, was
attended by leading
poets and intellectuals.*

Around this time the French artist Paul Éluard came to stay, along with his wife Gala. When they talked about the war, he and Max discovered they had both been at the Battle of Verdun on opposite sides, firing at each other, a revelation that underlined for them the obscenity and absurdity of the entire conflict. The two couples began to spend time together and it wasn't long before Luise was forced to accept that Max had fallen in love with Gala. Soon he announced he was going to Paris to live with Paul and Gala in a ménage à trois, leaving Luise and Maja to bring up little Jimmy. Luise must have been desperately upset but she wasn't bitter, telling her son in later life, "He was an unusual man, to whom the ordinary rules of life and behavior were less important than his work." Perhaps she also recognized the damage done to him by the war, which had made him capable of a selfishness and cruelty that had never been part of his nature before.

Luise and Jimmy stayed in Germany through the 1920s, during which time she became a respected art critic and intellectual, while Max lived in Paris and became a leading Surrealist artist who would marry four times altogether. After Hitler came to power in 1933 and the number of anti-Semitic laws grew ever larger and more oppressive, Luise came under suspicion from the regime

BELOW
Max Ernst (left) with Gala and Paul Éluard in Austria, 1922. In 1929 she fell in love with Spanish artist Salvador Dalí, ten years her junior, whom she married in 1934.

and hurriedly relocated to Paris. In 1938, as war seemed to be on the way, she sent her son Jimmy to New York, hoping to obtain a visa to follow him shortly afterwards. In 1939 she and Max were both living in the Marseille area, waiting for their American visas to come through, when the Second World War began. His visa was awarded because of his fame as an artist but there was no sign of hers, which appeared to be tied up in bureaucratic red tape. Max tried claiming to consular officials that their divorce had not been legal and that they were still married, thus entitling her to travel with him, but this argument was rejected. Max then offered to remarry Luise but she refused, pointing out that it would be nothing but a charade. In the end he sailed for New York without her and she went into hiding in the Alpes-Maritimes, staying with the renowned French author Jean Giorno. She felt optimistic, writing to her son "Even if the Germans came to Vichy, the peasants here revere this poet of their work and land so much that they would hide me from them.

... I'm in good hands." But sometime in 1943 or early 1944 she was captured by German soldiers occupying the area and sent to a Paris detention camp. On July 31, 1944, she was herded onto one of the last trains east to Auschwitz, and was killed in the gas chamber in the months before the camp was liberated in January 1945.

Max moved to the South of France in 1953 with his fourth wife, American Surrealist artist Dorothea Tanning, and they split their time between there and Paris. A major retrospective of his work was shown in New York and Paris in 1975. The following year, during the last weeks of his life as he lay in bed after a stroke, Max mused to his son Jimmy about Luise, calling her "a remarkable woman" and saying that of all his four wives, "Lou is the only woman . . . I ever thought of going back to." Theirs had been a strong, passionate love, a meeting of minds as well as a physical attraction, but in the end he had been too scarred by war for their relationship to work.

"Lou is the only woman ... I ever thought of going back to."

BELOW & RIGHT
*A handwritten draft of
"Violets," a poem Roland
wrote in April 1915.
He didn't send Vera a copy
till August that year as he
was still revising it, but that
April he did send her four
little violets gathered from
the roof of his dugout.*

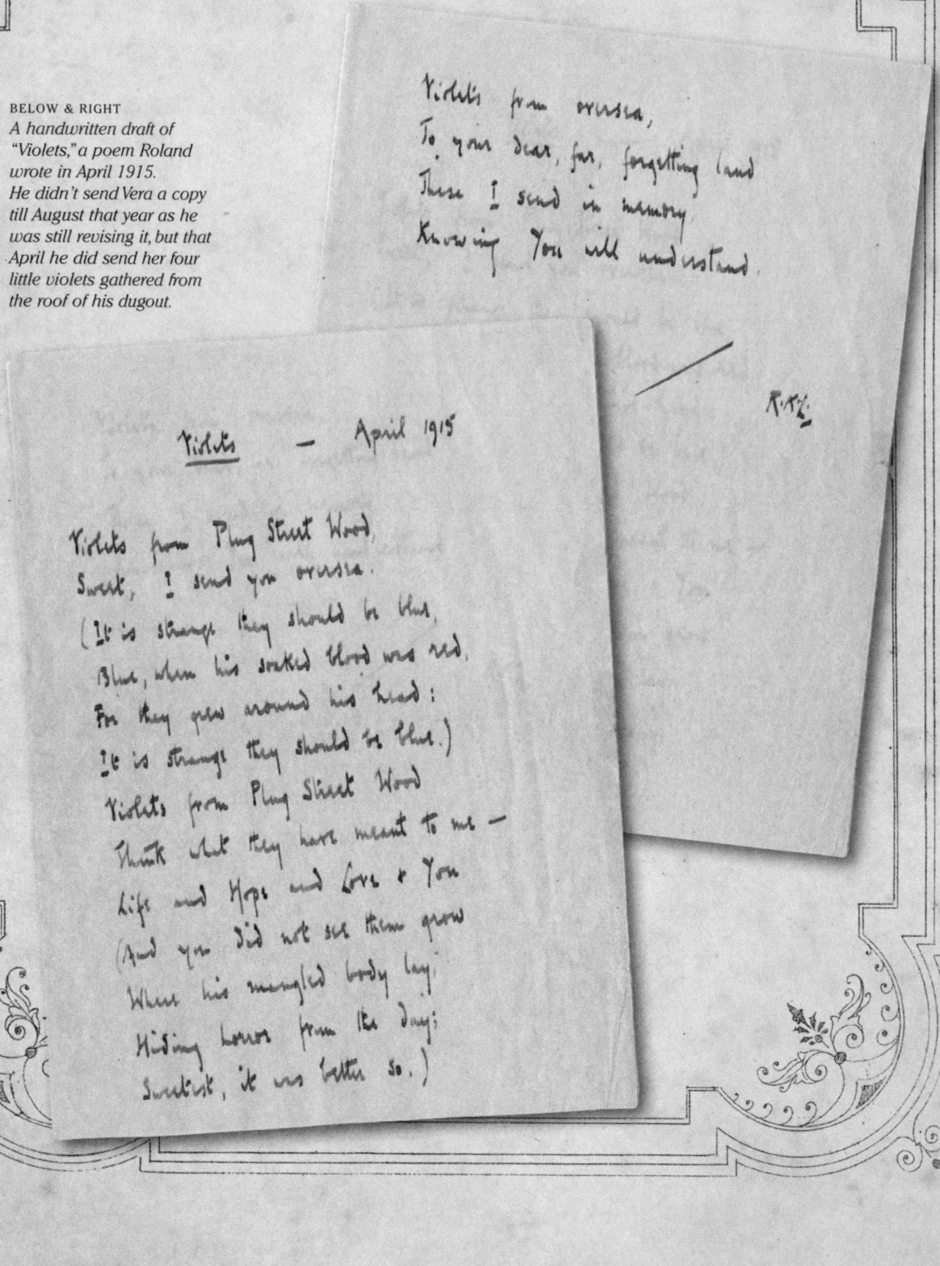

Violets from oversea,
To your dear, far, forgetting land
These I send in memory
Knowing You will understand.

R.A.L.

Violets — April 1915

Violets from Plug Street Wood,
Sweet, I send you oversea.
(It is strange they should be blue,
Blue, when his soaked blood was red,
For they grew around his head:
It is strange they should be blue.)
Violets from Plug Street Wood
Think what they have meant to me —
Life and Hope and Love & You
(And you did not see them grow
Where his mangled body lay,
Hiding horror from the day;
Sweetest, it was better so.)

Roland LEIGHTON
& Vera BRITTAIN

Roland Aubrey Leighton

BRITISH

Born: March 27, 1895

Rank & regiment:
Lieutenant, 7th Worcestershire
Regiment

Vera Mary Brittain

BRITISH

Born: December 29, 1893

War work:
Voluntary Aid Department
(VAD) nurse

ABOVE & RIGHT
Vera and Roland exchanged pictures in December 1914. He told her, "I should hate to go all through this War without being wounded at all; I should want something to prove that I had been in action."

WHEN ROLAND AND VERA MET IN APRIL 1914, THEY SOON
FOUND THEY WERE KINDRED SOULS, WITH A SHARED LOVE OF
LITERATURE AND PHILOSOPHY, AND THEY CONTINUED THEIR LONG
CONVERSATIONS IN LETTERS THAT BECAME INCREASINGLY DARK
AFTER HE ARRIVED AT THE WESTERN FRONT.

Both Vera and Roland came from well-to-do backgrounds. His father was literary editor of the *Daily Mail* and his mother wrote adventure novels for boys; her father was a paper-mill owner and her mother sang. They met because he was a close friend of her younger brother Edward at Uppingham School in Rutland. Edward invited him home to Buxton for the Easter holidays, and Vera wrote later that within ten minutes of meeting him she was impressed by his "maturity and sophistication." They spent the rest of the visit talking with each other about literature and religion, and he told her that at his mother's urging he had recently had his palm read by a man who warned him that in a year or two he ran "a considerable risk of assassination." They laughed it off, joking that his slight resemblance to the King of Portugal could provide the only possible motive!

LEFT
*According to Vera,
"At nineteen, Roland
looked twenty-four
and behaved with the
assurance of thirty …
his large dark eyes
looked contemplatively
at the world from
beneath black, strongly
marked eyebrows."*

Soon after the visit, Roland sent Vera a copy of a book they had discussed, by feminist writer Olive Schreiner, and Vera was delighted to find that he shared her feminist views. It was a critical time for her. She very much wanted to study at Oxford University, but her father believed that education for women was simply a preparation for marriage. Against his wishes, she had been working toward achieving the necessary qualifications, and Roland encouraged her. He himself planned to be there in autumn 1914, along with Edward, and that strengthened her resolve. She wrote in her diary that Roland "seems even in a short acquaintance to share both my faults and my talents and my ideas in a way that I have never found anyone else do yet."

They corresponded regularly and he sent her some of his poems, which she liked very much. Then in July they met again, when Vera came to his and her brother's school-leaving ceremony. She was impressed by the fact that Roland won almost every academic prize, but alarmed by the headmaster's jingoistic speech to the boys in which he said, "If a man can't serve his country, he's better dead." All the boys at Uppingham were in the Officers' Training Corps (OTC), which instilled in them a strong patriotism and a sense that they must do their duty.

Vera still had no inkling of the catastrophe that was about to be unleashed on the world. She had paid scant attention to the news stories about the assassination of Archduke Franz Ferdinand, and was merely looking forward to the autumn when they would all start at Oxford together. Roland was awarded the Classical Postmastership at Merton College and Vera managed to gain admittance to Somerville. And then war was declared and everything changed overnight.

Trying to get to the Front

Roland applied for a commission immediately, and Vera was relieved when he was turned down because of his less-than-perfect eyesight. However, he kept trying different regiments until at last he was accepted by one in Norwich. Her brother Edward obtained a commission with the 10th Sherwood Foresters. Only Vera would take her place at university that September, her excitement at attaining her goal tempered by anxiety over the safety of Edward and Roland. They were still only training, and she hoped against hope that they wouldn't be sent overseas.

In December 1914, she was able to meet Roland in London and felt shy seeing him again after their "months of intimate correspondence." He took her for tea with his mother and his sister Clare—his mother thoroughly approved of her—then at dinner that evening he gave her a beautiful bunch of tall pink roses. They were chaperoned by her aunt, but still managed to exchange a few affectionate words, and it was over that two-day period that Vera realized she had fallen in love with Roland—and that the feeling seemed to be mutual. After she left on New Year's Eve, he wrote that he felt wretched, and concluded, "You are a dear, you know."

ABOVE
The spires of Oxford University rise above the town; Vera, Roland, and Edward were looking forward to studying there in the fall of 1914.

Vera and Roland yearned to be alone together and contrived to escape the chaperones by meeting in Leicester and taking a train journey to Oxford, during which they made plans to travel together once the war was over. They admitted they had been keeping each other's letters, and he kissed her hand. After that their correspondence took on a new emotional intensity, marred only for Vera by Roland's desire to get to the Front. He felt ashamed still to be at home when men were coming back wounded, and in March 1915 he managed to obtain a transfer to the 7th Worcestershire, which was heading out to the Western Front. Vera rushed to London to see him off on the train, angry and worried by his decision, her heart filled with dread. He sent her an amethyst brooch as a keepsake, but she wrote expressing her doubts about the fighting: "Certainly war seems to bring out all that is noble in human nature, but against that you can say it brings out all the barbarous, too."

Her anxiety seemed misplaced at first, as Roland wrote that less than half an hour's walk from Armentières, where he was stationed, life carried on as normal. The trenches there were relatively quiet

at first, but in May he wrote that he had been under shellfire, and that "horror piled on horror till one feels that the world can scarcely go on any longer." Shortly after that, a man in his unit was killed. Roland had been speaking to him just moments earlier, walked off and when he came back found him lying in the bottom of the trench "with a tiny stream of blood trickling down his cheek into his coat." In a wood nearby he found the body of a soldier that must have lain there for some time, almost submerged in the moss and violets, an experience that became incorporated in "Villanelle," a poem he wrote for Vera that was destined to become one of his most famous: "It is strange they should be blue/ Blue when his soaked blood was red."

So as to do something for the war effort, Vera volunteered to help at a local hospital and was initially set to darning socks. In June 1915 she arranged to take time off from university and started working at the Devonshire Hospital, where she was kept frantically busy emptying bedpans and changing dressings. She tried to remain positive in her letters to Roland, to boost his flagging morale: "Even War must end sometime, and perhaps … we may recover the hidden childhood again and find that after all the dust and ashes which covered it haven't spoilt it much." But he was gloomy. Recalling their last evening together, he wrote, "It all seems so far away now. I sometimes think I must have exchanged my life for someone else's."

In August he came home on leave, looking thinner and older. They planned to visit her family and then his, but balked at the chaperones dictated by the age. "Would it make things better if we were properly engaged?" Roland asked shyly. Vera argued that she did not want her relationship to be labeled as one that society saw as "correct," and dreaded the conventional congratulations and advice from their elders. Her feminist ideals meant she didn't want to give her father the opportunity to quiz Roland on how he planned to support her, since she had long ago decided that she would work and be financially independent. She didn't want a ring, which she saw as a "token of possession." Roland agreed with her and they decided not to tell her parents of their engagement until after that visit. When she did break the news, no one was surprised. Edward remarked, "You're only giving a name to what has existed for quite a long time."

All too soon, it was time for Vera to get back to her work in the hospital. They kissed as Roland saw her off on the train and tears welled up in his eyes that he struggled to hide. Each had promised they would not look back after saying farewell, but she turned to watch him walking quickly down the platform with his head bent and shoulders hunched.

> "*It all seems such a waste of youth, such a desecration of all that is born for beauty and poetry.*"

Back in the Trenches

Roland's initial enthusiasm for fighting was utterly extinguished by the horror of the trenches that autumn: "Let him who thinks War is a glorious, golden thing ... look at a little pile of sodden grey rags that cover half a skull and a shin-bone and what might have been Its ribs," he wrote to Vera.

She got work at a VAD military hospital in Camberwell in London, where she changed dressings on gangrenous wounds and amputation stumps, and helped men suffering from shellshock. It was tough, distressing work, but still she tried to stay positive; in fact, she and Roland quarreled by letter over his negativity. In November he wrote, "It all seems such a waste of youth, such a desecration of all that is born for beauty and poetry," even questioning whether it would have been better if they had never met, or at least had not met until after the war was over. He told Vera she seemed to him like a character in a book, and she admitted in her diary that she couldn't visualize his face any more.

And then word came that Roland would get leave over Christmas. It was just what the couple

THE VADS

The Voluntary Aid Detachment (VAD) was formed in 1909 by both male and female volunteers, but during the war it was mostly staffed by women, as the men were fighting. They worked in military hospitals both at home and overseas, providing support to the medical staff, but the fact that they were not fully qualified nurses caused some resentment at first. As the war went on and they gained experience, they were more welcome and proved invaluable, with about 38,000 VADs helping with the war effort on the Western and later on the Eastern Front. Several women who served as VADs went on to become famous. Apart from Vera Brittain, there were Agatha Christie, popular mystery story writer; Amelia Earhart, the pioneering aviator; and Freya Stark, the explorer and travel writer.

RIGHT
British VAD dressing station: The matron sits at the back supervising while a nurse dresses a wound on a soldier's hand.

needed, so she made sure she was able to take a week off work at the same time. On Christmas Eve 1915, she helped to decorate the ward at her hospital, then on Christmas morning took a train to Brighton, where she had arranged to meet Roland in the lounge at the Grand Hotel after his boat train arrived. There was no sign of him by ten o'clock that night, so she assumed, since it was Christmas Day, that there had been problems with transport. The following morning she was called to the hotel telephone and she rushed to answer, expecting to hear his voice. Instead it was that of his sister Clare, saying that Roland was not coming. He had been shot through the stomach while repairing the barbed wire in front of his trench, and had died in a military hospital on December 23.

Over the following weeks, Vera received letters from his fellow officers and a Catholic priest who had buried him, explaining what had happened in Roland's final hours. His unit had taken over an old trench, which was in pretty bad shape, and not one of the previous occupants had thought to warn them that the Germans had a machine gun

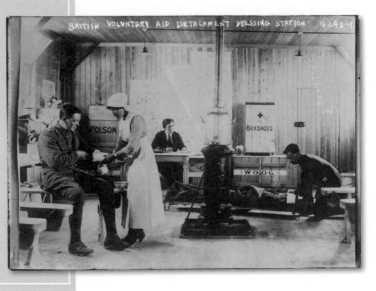

trained on a gap in the hedge at the exact point where the wire was torn. When Roland crawled out in the moonlight, he was hit immediately. No purpose had been served by his death. Not one other life had been saved. He was simply gone.

Vera visited Roland's family at their home in January just as a package arrived containing his belongings, including the uniform he had been wearing when shot—"the tunic torn back and front by the bullet, a khaki vest dark and stiff with blood"—and felt sheer rage at the gruesome awfulness of the war.

She returned to work in Camberwell, utterly grief-stricken but determined to keep herself busy. On top of the strain of losing her fiancé, news came that her brother Edward had arrived at the Western Front in February, from where he wrote to her of the hazards of "stray shots that ricochet off a sandbag" and the dangers of going out on patrol in no-man's-land. On July 1 he was shot in the thigh and arm at the Battle of the Somme and sent back to London. Vera arrived at work to be told her brother was in J Ward and, filled with relief, she dashed there to see him. He received a military cross for

BELOW
No-man's-land: Roland wrote "The dug-outs have nearly all blown in, the wire entanglements are a wreck, and in the chaos of twisted iron and splintered timber and shapeless earth are the fleshless, blackened bones of simple men."

WAR CEMETERIES

The scale of military casualties in the First World War was utterly unprecedented, with some estimating that as many as 10 million were killed. Those who died in hospitals were placed in a cemetery nearby, and the location was generally registered, as it was for Edward Brittain and Roland Leighton. However, as the fighting moved back and forth with increasing fierceness, thousands were buried where they fell, with perhaps a basic cross or marker, and some simply remained on the ground to be covered in mud, like the soldier Roland found in the wood. After the war, families wanted to visit their loved ones' graves and many of the fighting nations established a registration service. Where no grave could be found, the missing were listed on memorials, and both war cemeteries and memorials are maintained to this day.

RIGHT
Edward Brittain's gravestone in Granezza, just south of Asiago, in northern Italy.

BELOW
There are over a hundred military cemeteries in Belgium, containing the remains of soldiers of many different nationalities.

his valor at the Somme, but after a few months, as soon as his wounds had healed, he was sent back to the Front to fight.

Wanting to prove herself worthy of Roland, Vera volunteered to serve as a VAD overseas and was sent to Malta, where she cared for patients whose ships had been blown up in the surrounding waters, before going on to Étaples in France, where she found herself nursing acutely ill German soldiers, some with suppurating blisters caused by mustard gas. Such was their suffering, she saw them only as human beings, not as the enemy.

In June 1918 Edward was sent to the Italian Front, where his luck finally ran out. He was shot in the head by a sniper on June 15, 1918, and died instantly. This was the loss that truly broke Vera's heart. On Armistice Day, she struggled through the crowds in London, thinking of "gifted, ardent, ambitious" Roland, who died doing a task of routine maintenance; of "musical, serene" Edward, who loved peace but had fought so courageously.

After the war, Vera finished her degree at Oxford, and lived a long life as a celebrated author of novels and memoirs, including the bestselling *Testament of Youth*. She also spoke at peace rallies and was a prominent member of the Peace Pledge Union. She married and had two children, but asked that when she died her ashes be scattered on her brother's grave in the Italian hills, "because for nearly 50 years my heart has been in that Italian village cemetery." Roland's grave in the military cemetery of Louvencourt in France is covered in violets, in memory of the poem he wrote for Vera back in 1915.

ABOVE
Edward Brittain's medal for gallantry, earned at the Somme in 1916.

TOP
Vera in the 1920s: Her first novel, The Dark Tide, *was published in 1923.*

> " *... for nearly 50 years my heart has been in that Italian village cemetery.* "

Yanks going into action
France

The British and French
were delighted when
America entered the
war, but it took a long
time before US troops
reached the front line.

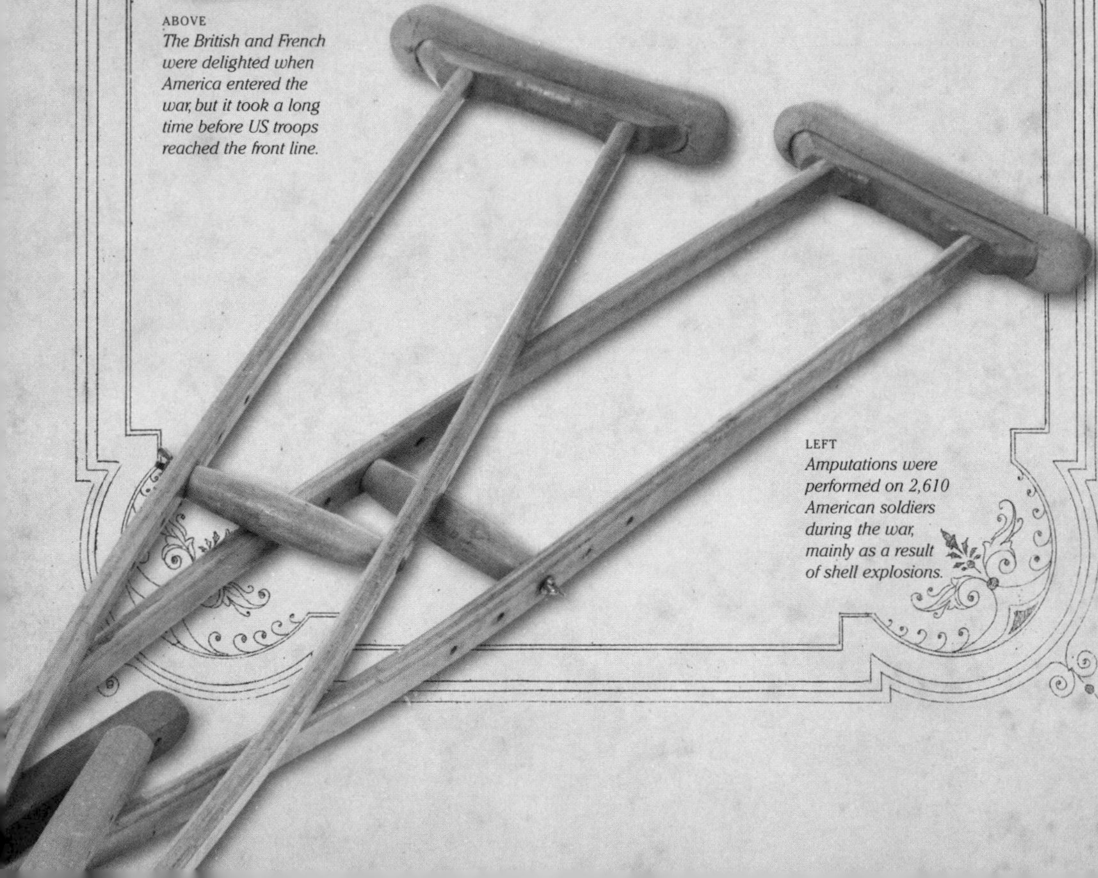

Amputations were
performed on 2,610
American soldiers
during the war,
mainly as a result
of shell explosions.

Charlie & Valentine
BOUCHER

Married: October 13, 1919

Charles Leo Boucher
FRENCH-CANADIAN

Born: February 13, 1894

Rank & regiment:
Sergeant, 102nd Infantry,
26th US Division

Valentine Antoinette Breton
FRENCH

Born: November 1, 1897

ABOVE
*Charlie Boucher photographed
in 1917 before leaving for
Europe. He had a taste for
adventure from a young age.*

CHARLIE ALWAYS THOUGHT OF HIMSELF AS A LUCKY MAN, BUT THE LUCKIEST MOMENT OF HIS LIFE WOULD COME NEAR THE WAR'S END WHEN HE SAW A BEAUTIFUL YOUNG FRENCH GIRL STANDING NEAR A WELL. HE FELL FOR HER ON THE SPOT.

Charlie came from a long line of French immigrants who had settled in Quebec in the early 17th century. His father, a carpenter in Providence, Rhode Island, was fatally injured in an accident at work when Charlie was only a month old. His mother took him, his two brothers, and his sister back to live on her father's farm in Drummondville, Quebec, but Charlie didn't learn to speak much French at home because his grandfather was a loyalist who ran an English-speaking household. When he was in his late teens, his mother moved the family to the Boston area where there was more work available, and in 1913 Charlie enlisted for the Second Corps of Cadets of Salem in search of adventure.

If not adventure, his army career did at least serve up a few scary moments when in June 1916 his company were rushed down to Arizona to help protect the border with Mexico after an attack on a US garrison by rebels led by Pancho Villa. For one thing, he was extremely lucky when, having captured a large lizard and put a string round his neck to keep it as a pet, a Mexican prisoner warned him that the lizard was in fact a Gila monster with a fierce bite and a poison more deadly than a rattlesnake's. He also had a close shave when a Mexican sentry guard almost spotted him after he had sneaked across the border to do some sightseeing, but he managed to return unharmed. It was then he began to think of himself as "Lucky Charlie."

Soon after his return to Boston, in February 1917, Charlie was put on duty guarding railroad lines and bridges along the Connecticut River as there were fears after America entered the war that German agents might try to dynamite them. In another stroke of good fortune, he had a near miss one evening when a friend came in from guard duty with numb fingers from the freezing winter cold and accidentally discharged his rifle, the bullet grazing Charlie's head. Charlie was fine, but the friend went into shock!

... he began to think of himself as "Lucky Charlie."

Rumors spread through the ranks that they would shortly be sent to Europe, but it wasn't until September 20, 1917, that they set sail from the Canadian port city of Montreal. They were ordered to wear lifejackets at all times in case of a torpedo strike from a German U-boat, and indeed just two days away from the Irish coast they were startled by a number of explosions that rocked the ship. Charlie and his friends rushed up on deck about to leap overboard but were told the explosions had been gunner practice between the destroyers who accompanied them. They docked in Liverpool, then Southampton, and arrived in Le Havre on October 16, after which they traveled by train and on foot up to the Vosges Mountains for training in operating the new French machine guns and grenades. The British and French soldiers grumbled about the inexperienced Americans landing on French soil, but in fact they were delighted to have the "Yanks" join them in facing the Germans. The boost to morale was immense, as was the corresponding dent in the morale of German troops.

BELOW
The Battle of Seicheprey began with a raid by German crack troops designed to intimidate the Americans, who were untried in battle. At least eighty of Charlie's division were killed that day.

The Battle of Seicheprey

It wasn't long before Charlie's company saw action as they moved up through Nancy and Verdun to the Soissons area. Some of the men were wounded by shellfire or struck down by gas attacks, but

SEICHEPREY, THE SCENE OF THE FIRST

there were no replacements
available, and he complained
in a memoir he wrote after the
war that there was very little
food to go around. One night
Charlie managed to get lost
among the hordes of Allied
troops—British, French, and
Italian—near the chalk mines
of Soissons, and was pleased
to be invited by a French
sergeant to eat a hearty meal
he had cooked to celebrate
a friend's promotion, before
rejoining his men.

ABOVE
*Men of Charlie's division,
the 102nd, line up to have
their clothes disinfected.
Lice laid eggs in the
seams of garments and
it was hard to get rid
of them.*

On the night of April 19, 1918, Charlie was called to an emergency
meeting in a dugout behind the lines where American officers
were told that French intelligence had picked up reports of a
planned German attack on their position. Charlie and his men
were ordered to advance to an exposed spot which, as he later
wrote in his memoir, "proved to be a suicide post." As the Germans
stormed their position, Charlie and his men mowed several down

N BATTLE, APRIL 20. 1918.

TUNNELERS

A key tactic in trench warfare was digging tunnels under no-man's-land then setting off huge caches of dynamite directly beneath enemy lines. The Germans tried it first in December 1914 when they wiped out an entire Indian brigade in Belgium, and the French and British were quick to follow suit, bringing in specialist teams of miners. The men worked in silence, listening for signs of enemy tunnelers, while conditions underground were dark, cold, and lacking in oxygen. It could take as long as a year to dig a tunnel and position a mine, but when it worked the tactic was spectacularly successful. In 1917, over 8,000 metres of tunnel and 600 tons of explosive were placed in position under German trenches at Messines. When these were exploded at 3:10 p.m. on June 7, 1917, 10,000 German soldiers were killed in an explosion so loud that it was heard all the way back in London. By the time Charlie arrived at the Front, tunneling was less used because the front lines were moving more frequently, but he wandered into the chalk mines at Soissons through a camouflaged entrance and saw "thousands of lights and routes leading in every direction."

with machine-gun fire and killed yet more in hand-to-hand combat, but they were heavily outnumbered. In fact, the German troops turned out to be highly trained Prussian shock troops sent to terrorize the untested Americans in the outlying forward positions. Charlie was wounded early on the morning of April 20 by a piece of shrapnel that struck him in the leg but, having made a tourniquet from a shoelace and a piece of duckboard, he managed to continue fighting. One by one, his men were cut down around him. At nightfall, Charlie managed to crawl back through no-man's-land toward his outfit, taking with him a wounded comrade, George Cooper. From his original platoon of sixty men, he found there were only eight left alive, all of them badly wounded. The Battle of Seicheprey, as this

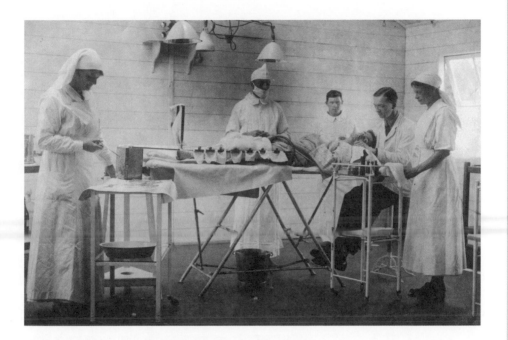

became known, was one of the earliest battles fought by the
American Expeditionary Force and was generally considered
a success for the Americans, although the death toll was high.
The boys from Connecticut had held their "suicide post"; though,
as Charlie said, "Oh! God! At what a price!"

ABOVE
*Field surgeons had to
learn how to treat
appalling wounds that
were contaminated
by bacteria from the
unsanitary conditions
at the front line.*

A Long Recuperation

George Cooper died on a stretcher alongside Charlie's while they
waited for an ambulance to take them to the hospital at Toul. Charlie
was sedated, but on arrival he dimly overheard surgeons talking
about amputating his leg and he yelled and cried out in his sleep
as if still fighting in the trenches. He was moved again and woke up
in the Ritz Carlton Hotel in Vichy, which was operating as a hospital.
There were palm trees alongside his bed and he could just make
out the shimmering outline of the city through his window. It was
there he learned that he had sustained a fourteen-inch wound
in his leg through which gangrene had set in. Moreover, he had
suffered chlorine gas burns to his eyes and a burst left eardrum
from the shellfire. The decision was made to move him to an
American hospital near Bordeaux. Here they treated his wound
with an antiseptic solution called Dakin's fluid, which had just

OPPOSITE
*French tunnelers digging
under a German trench,
c.1916. They had to work
in utter silence to avoid
detection.*

> "Gee ... that girl is going to make some man a wonderful wife. She is as cute and neat as a pin."

been developed for use on infected wounds. Charlie was desperate to avoid amputation, because the survival rate after the operation seemed to be very low, and fortunately the Dakin's Fluid began to work. Then Spanish Flu hit the hospital, causing an average of 25 deaths every day at the height of the epidemic. Somehow Charlie managed to avoid it. His luck was holding.

As soon as he could get about on crutches, he set out on little daily walks. The hospital was at the foot of a hill on which sat the town of Montignac and one day he hobbled up to the town, wearing only a pair of French army pajamas and a terrycloth bathrobe. A group of local people were chatting near a well, and his eye was caught by a French girl wearing a plaid skirt and white blouse. "Gee," he thought to himself, "that girl is going to make some man a wonderful wife. She is as cute and neat as a pin."

A few days later when he walked up to the town again, he noticed the girl and her mother sitting sewing outside their house, and this time Charlie tried out a few French words, with the aid of a French–English dictionary he had brought along. The women produced a chair for him and poured a glass of wine, and he learned that the girl's name was Valentine. She worked as a dressmaker, having been trained by her uncle, a professional tailor. She and her mother were living with relatives after her father's death at the front line earlier in the war. Up close she was even more beautiful than he'd thought, and Charlie began walking up to Montignac every day to sit with her and her mother. The relationship was entirely chaste and proper, but the two were strongly drawn to each other. Their secret smiles and long looks were as eloquent as any declaration of love. Shyly, Charlie suggested to Valentine that they might be married one day when his wounds had healed and she blushed and nodded her agreement. Valentine's mother liked Charlie and was happy to give her permission for them to wed.

Not long after this a contingent of troops from Kentucky arrived in Montignac, and after a couple of fights in the town between the Southerners from Kentucky and the Yankees in the hospital, Montignac was declared out of bounds. Guards were even placed on the road, but Charlie borrowed some civilian clothes from a cousin of Valentine's and, with his rudimentary French, managed to persuade the guards to let him pass so he could continue to see the girl he had fallen for. But then orders came that the hospital was to be evacuated and Charlie was told his war was over. He would not be returning to the fighting, but would be sent back to America on the next available hospital ship. Valentine's mother cooked a special dinner for him on the last night, addresses were exchanged, and they said their sad farewells. Valentine prayed he wouldn't forget her once he was back in America; she considered them to be engaged, but had no idea when—or if—they might be able to tie the knot.

Homeward Bound

Two days after the Armistice, Charlie sailed on the *Orizaba* bound for New York. His mother and two brothers came and joined him for a Thanksgiving dinner in a New York hospital. Over the next ten months he had to endure a number of operations as bone specialists reconstructed his damaged leg, removing splinters of bone, shrapnel, and scar tissue, then putting skin grafts over the wound site. The time passed slowly, but he focused on improving his French and writing letters to Valentine. She replied, keeping her language as simple as possible so he could understand her.

LEFT
The Orizaba had been a cargo ship before the war, and as a hospital ship without any cargo below deck she became top-heavy and pitched and rolled badly while Charlie was on his way back to the US.

WARTIME MEDICAL ADVANCES

New measures were taken to combat infectious diseases during the war, including the development of a typhoid vaccine, and tetanus shots. A lot was discovered about wound management in field hospitals. Doctors learned not to close a wound where there was contamination but to keep it open and regularly trim infected tissue while using antiseptic solutions to clean it, as happened with Charlie Boucher. Orthopaedic surgeons pioneered new methods of amputation and bone reconstruction, while artificial limbs became more effective. Neurosurgeons learned about treating wounds that affected the central nervous system after fractures to vertebrae, and the art of facial reconstruction was pioneered to help pilots who had crawled away from the wrecks of their planes alive but badly burned. This led to the founding of the American Association of Plastic Surgeons in 1921. At first plastic surgeons refused to perform surgery for cosmetic reasons, but by the 1930s attitudes had changed and nose jobs were all the rage in America, followed in the late 1940s by facelifts.

Still there was a possibility his leg might be amputated, an outcome he dreaded, and he wrote to Valentine that if that should happen he would never think of getting married. He suggested that if any local young men coming back from the war should ask for her hand, she should not hesitate on his account. But, he promised, as soon as he was discharged from hospital he would come to visit her. Valentine replied, saying that she hoped he would not lose his leg but even if he did, they would get by just fine so long as he still cared for her. She sent him a photograph of herself which became one of his most prized possessions.

In the summer of 1919 Charlie was discharged from the army. His right foot would always be semi-paralyzed, he had damaged corneas in both eyes, and was deaf in his left ear, but he could walk, albeit with a pronounced limp. He was entitled to a monthly disability payment from the army but before he settled down, his mother urged him to go back to Montignac for the lovely French girl he never stopped

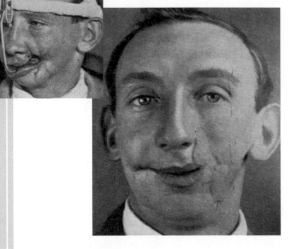

ABOVE
The facial reconstruction of a soldier who was wounded in July 1916 during the Battle of the Somme.

talking about. He sailed on September 13, 1919, sending Valentine a cablegram from the ship; she was waiting for him when he arrived in Montignac. They went to the mayor's office to file the necessary papers, waited two weeks for the banns to be read in church and then, on Monday, October 13, 1919, the mayor pronounced them man and wife in a ceremony at the Hôtel de Ville (town hall). The following morning there was a church wedding after which the entire town of Montignac turned out for the wedding feast. Tables made of planks of wood lined the streets, and several courses were served: chicken, veal, beef, lamb, and side dishes, accompanied by wine and liqueurs.

ABOVE
Valentine, Charlie, Wilfred, and Edith in 1924. The family twice went back to France to visit, once when the children were young and again when they were in their teens.

When Charlie and Valentine sailed back to the States, Valentine's mother came with them. They set up home in New Haven, Connecticut, where Charlie got a well-paid job as a postal supervisor. For the first few years of marriage, Valentine regularly had to change the dressings on his wounded leg, and she also comforted him when he had nightmares about the battles he had witnessed. In 1920 they had a daughter, Edith, and in 1922 a son, Wilfred. French was the main language spoken in the household, so the children grew up bilingual and absorbed their mother's love of arts and culture. Valentine observed many French traditions, such as preparing French meals with a salad following the entrée, and she always enjoyed browsing through French fashion magazines.

The couple's marriage lasted sixty years and in time they were able to enjoy nine grandchildren. Valentine was everything Charlie had imagined she would be when he saw her standing by the well in Montignac—and more, as she turned out to be a wonderful homemaker and an inspiring mother to their children. Some question whether love at first sight can turn into true love that will last, but for Lucky Charlie that was definitely the case.

IN THE NAME OF MERCY
GIVE !

© HERBERT HERTER

GREETINGS FROM
AMERICAN RED CROSS
CANTEEN SERVICE

ABOVE
*A Red Cross fundraising poster, c.1918.
The international organization was
awarded the Nobel Peace Prize in 1917
for its outstanding work during the war.*

Ernest
HEMINGWAY
&
Agnes von
KUROWSKY

Ernest Miller Hemingway

AMERICAN

Born: July 21, 1899

War work:
Red Cross ambulance driver

Agnes von Kurowsky

AMERICAN

Born: January 5, 1892

War work:
Red Cross nurse

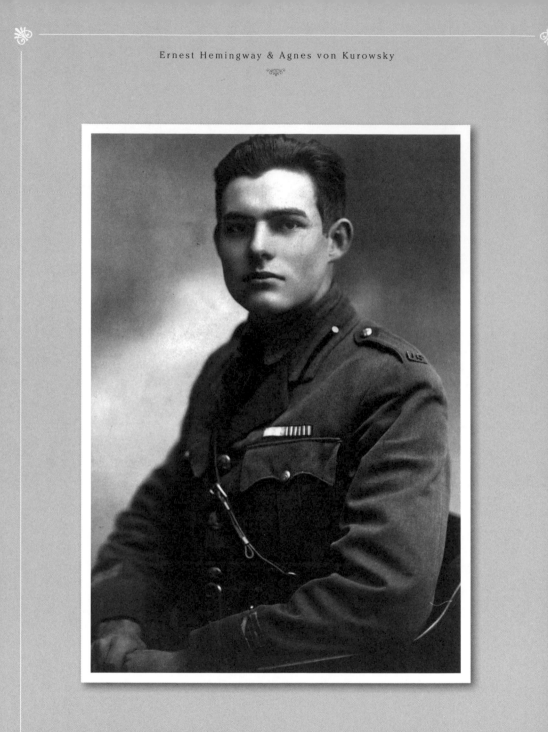

ABOVE
*At the age of nineteen, Hemingway
was good-looking, with an extrovert
character, but he could be rude and
uncooperative with his nurses—
apart from Agnes.*

"IT DOES BEAT ALL HOW POPULAR I HAVE BECOME IN THE LAST SIX MOS," WROTE AGNES IN HER DIARY. "MUST BE BECAUSE I'M TURNING FRIVOLOUS." AMONG THE HEARTS SHE STOLE WHILE WORKING IN MILAN AS A RED CROSS NURSE WAS THAT OF AN IMPRESSIONABLE YOUNG AMBULANCE DRIVER NAMED ERNEST HEMINGWAY.

P olish-German-Russian by descent, Paul Moritz Julius von Kurowsky arrived in the US from Königsberg, Germany, in 1890 and settled in Washington, DC, where he taught languages at the Berlitz school. It was in Washington that he met and married Agnes's mother, Agnes Theodosia Holabird. The family moved around a lot during Agnes's childhood, staying in Alaska and Vancouver, but Washington became home by the time she was a teenager. Agnes attended the Fairmount Seminary for young ladies, and after her father's early death, when she was just eighteen years old, she took a job in the catalogue department of the Carnegie Library. "That was too slow and uneventful," she later told friends. "My taste ran to something more exciting." She trained as a nurse at Bellevue Hospital in New York and applied for an overseas Red Cross assignment as soon as she graduated. She was perhaps inspired to do her duty by her family's strong military history—both her grandfathers had served as generals in their country's forces—

BELOW
Agnes and Ernest (center) with two other nurses at Milan's San Siro racetrack in 1918. "He is adorable & we are congenial in every way," Agnes wrote in her diary.

> *"She had a sparkle the others didn't possess. Fresh and pert and lovely in her long-skirted white uniform ... she radiated zest and energy."*

or perhaps she was just looking for some fun. On June 15, 1918, she sailed for Europe on the *SS La Lorraine*. She was twenty-six years old.

Agnes was very attractive, with chestnut hair and blue-grey eyes, and her cheerful persona was popular with men. She had already dated several beaus before she left America, and she left a man known in her diary as "Dr. S" under the impression that they had a commitment, but she still enjoyed flirting with Belgian officers during the Atlantic crossing and according to her diary one Lt. Collins gave her "souvenirs" every day and her friends warned her not to break his heart. On arrival in Milan she was reunited with a group of nurses she had known at Bellevue, and soon met her next beau—Captain Enrico Serena of the Italian army—at a Red Cross event near Lake Maggiore. She began work at the Italian hospital in Milan, then the new Red Cross hospital in Milan opened on July 17, 1918. Agnes reported for work just as a eighteen-year-old boy named Ernest Hemingway was being brought in on a stretcher.

According to Henry Villard, a Red Cross driver who was there at the same time, all the patients fell for Agnes: "She had a sparkle the others didn't possess. Fresh and pert and lovely in her long-skirted white uniform . . . she radiated zest and energy." Under Red Cross rules, unchaperoned contact between the sexes was strictly forbidden, but Agnes had never been the type of girl to let a rule stand in the way of a good time.

BELOW
The schoolboy Hemingway at age sixteen, a year before America entered the war. His family was disappointed when he decided not to go to college but to seek work as a reporter instead.

A Young Man's First Love

Ernest Hemingway grew up in Oak Park, Illinois, the son of a physician father and musician mother who owned comfortable homes both in town and on Walloon Lake, Michigan, where as a young boy Ernest learned to hunt and fish. He did well at school, particularly in English, and decided to make a career as a journalist. His first job was as a cub reporter at the Kansas City Star, but he had only been there for six months when there was a Red Cross recruitment drive in

AMERICAN PUBLIC OPINION OF THE WAR

In 1914, almost all Americans felt they should stay out of the war in Europe. Irish Americans were hostile to the idea of helping the British after the 1916 Easter Uprising (Ireland's rebellion against British rule) had been brutally crushed by British forces. German Americans were understandably keen for the US to stay neutral. Midwestern farmers cared only about the price their crops could get in market and were concerned this could be affected in wartime. Women and clergymen throughout the US argued for a negotiated peace, and peace movements were formed, such as Andrew Carnegie's Endowment for International Peace, established to advance cooperation between nations. But the sinking of the *Lusitania* by a torpedo from a German U-boat in May 1915 with the loss of 1,195 passengers, including 128 Americans, began to sway public opinion. The Germans agreed to halt their unrestricted submarine warfare in the Atlantic, but when they resumed it in January 1917 and eight US ships were sunk in February and March, Woodrow Wilson felt he had no choice but to involve US forces. He'd been elected in November 1916 on the slogan, "He kept us out of war," but on April 4, 1917 the US declared war on Germany.

RIGHT
Woodrow Wilson tried hard to keep America out of the war.

BELOW
RMS Lusitania *was sunk 11.5 miles off Kinsale Head on the south coast of Ireland*

> ⁶⁶ *My country needed me, and I went and did whatever I was told.* ⁹⁹

TOP
Hemingway in a Red Cross ambulance in Italy in June 1918. He only served there for a few weeks.

town for which he signed up in April 1917. "My country needed me, and I went and did whatever I was told," he later explained to his hometown newspaper.

He left the US in May 1918 and sailed to Paris—at the time being bombarded by German troops—and in June 1918 was dispatched to the Italian Front, just as Austro-Hungarian troops launched an attack on the Italian army near Lake Maggiore. However, things were relatively quiet in the area where Hemingway was assigned to work as an ambulance driver. He soon got bored with the routine and volunteered for the rolling canteen service that dispensed drinks, cigarettes, and chocolate to soldiers along the front line. He was transferred to the canteen at Fossalta, a village by the Piave River, and soon realized how dangerous the area was when another rolling canteen driver was killed by an Austrian shell. Sure enough, Hemingway had been there just six days when on July 8 a trench mortar exploded right next to him. A man standing beside him was killed and several others wounded. Hemingway's legs were "pretty smashed up," but he managed to carry another of the wounded to safety, though not without being hit in the foot and knee by machine-gun bullets—"like a sharp smack on the leg with an icy snowball," he wrote to his parents.

He spent five days in a field hospital and was then taken by train to Milan and admitted to the American Red Cross hospital. They found 237 wounds in his legs, with pieces of shrapnel buried inside the flesh and bullets lodged in his knee and foot. Although most wounds were superficial, the knee and foot required surgery and Hemingway worried that he might have to lose a leg. Fortunately, the operation was a success and he was given one of the bullets as a souvenir, but he was also told he needed several weeks of recuperation during which he could not get out of bed.

Hemingway was in the room next to Henry Villard and the doors were left open, so the two soon became firm friends, but his main focus of interest was the lovely Agnes von Kurowsky, who often worked night shifts and liked to party with her patients. On Hemingway's birthday, July 21, they played the Victrola (an early record player), ate ice cream, and drank a large bottle of cognac on the balcony. On August 13, she brought in a mandolin so the patients could have musical evenings, and they often played poker. By August 25, Hemingway was so seriously smitten that she wrote about it in her diary: "Ernest Hemingway has a case on me . . . he is a dear boy & so cute about it." On August 31, the first day he was able to get out of bed, she let him take her out for dinner and buy a bottle of her favorite Asti Spumante. And although they tried to keep it secret, Henry Villard noticed them holding hands "in a manner that did not suggest she was taking his pulse." On September 11, Agnes gave her "home ring" to Hemingway—whom she called "the Kid"—in what she later called "a gesture to solidify the friendship." Captain Serena was out of

ROLLING CANTEENS

During the war, the Red Cross had many roles: transporting the wounded, looking after servicemen in hospitals and convalescent homes, ferrying humanitarian supplies into war zones, and helping families to get word of wounded or missing relatives. One of their most popular initiatives was the rolling canteen that took supplies to soldiers on the front line. At first these were trailers that could be hauled along behind the lines, but this proved difficult in areas such as the north of Italy where roads were impassable, so some of them developed into static huts situated at crossroads that the troops frequently passed. They would be decorated with patriotic posters and might even have a phonograph and a collection of records—and they served treats: jam, croissants, chocolate, and hot and cold drinks. It was a huge morale booster for battle-weary troops to have a rolling canteen arrive in their vicinity.

LEFT
American Red Cross volunteers tended to be well-educated men from wealthy backgrounds.

the picture now and Hemingway laughingly told her off for "being mean to the Capitano," little expecting that such a fate might one day be his.

There's no doubt that Agnes and Hemingway became very close over the next month. Quite how close has always been a matter of conjecture, with him implying they had a sexual relationship. He told friends, "It takes a trained nurse to make love to a man with one leg in a splint." But although her yellow hairpin was found under his pillow one day, it seems unlikely she did more than embrace the man for whom she evidently felt increasing tenderness. The open-door policy alone would have made it difficult for the young couple to get any privacy. Still, on October 15, Agnes was suddenly transferred to work in a hospital in Florence and wrote to Hemingway just after her arrival, "I kept wishing I had you alongside of me, so I could put my head on that nice place—you know—the hollow place for my face—& go to sleep with your arm around me."

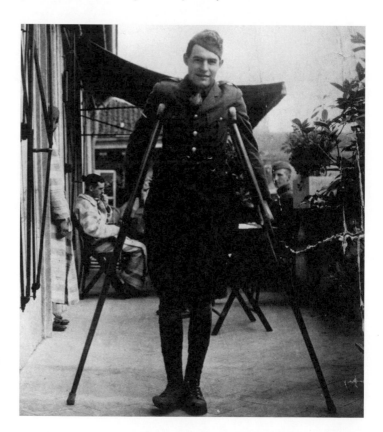

RIGHT
*According to Hemingway,
"The 237 wounds I got
from the trench mortar
didn't hurt a bit ...
[but] my kneecap was
acting queer."*

Hemingway returned briefly to the Front in late October, but succumbed to hepatitis and was back in a hospital bed when the war ended on November 11. He waited anxiously every day to see if a letter would arrive from Agnes, and pined when he didn't hear. Absence intensified their romance and by December they were talking about getting married. Hemingway met her in Treviso on December 9, and four days later she wrote to her mother that she was "planning to marry a man younger than I—& it wasn't a Doctor." Hemingway certainly believed they were engaged to be married and although he didn't tell his parents, he had written to his mother on August 29 to say he was in love; on his return to the US just before Christmas, with an honorable discharge from the Army, he also told friends of his forthcoming marriage.

The Brush-off

It's obvious from Agnes's letters to Hemingway that she cared deeply about him, but the issue of age comes up time and again: "When you add on a few years & some dignity & calm, you'll be very much worth while," she writes to him, and persists in calling him "Kid." At the same time, she mentions that a friend has called her "a flirt" and writes on December 31, "Capt. Moore was teasing me today about my fondness for Italian officers," which can't have gone down well with her betrothed. His letters to her have not survived, but presumably he was anxious for them to be reunited and to name the day. He had no idea that her feelings for him were cooling until he received her letter of March 7, in which she

> " *...I am still very fond of you, but, it is more as a mother than as a sweetheart.* "

BELOW
The wedding of Hemingway and Hadley Richardson on September 3, 1921. Their marriage would last just five years before she realized he was involved with another woman.

dropped a bombshell: "I know that I am still very fond of you, but, it is more as a mother than as a sweetheart." In case he should still have hope of changing her mind, she added, almost casually, "I expect to be married soon." Back in January, she had begun to date an Italian nobleman called Domenico Caracciolo, and it had quickly become serious.

Hemingway was utterly devastated. He took to bed at his parents' home and told a friend, "I'm just smashed by it . . . I forgot all about religion and everything else because I had [her] to worship." The medals he received for his bravery in the Piave River campaign did nothing to heal his pain. He never saw Agnes again and if he wrote in response to her heartbreaking letter, she did not reply. In 1922, after he had married another woman, Hadley Richardson, he wrote to let her know. "It is so nice to feel I have an old friend back," she replied, in a long, newsy letter. But she wasn't at all pleased when Hemingway began to publish short stories with

characters that bore striking similarities to her. His first major success, a 1929 novel called *A Farewell to Arms*, was about an American Red Cross ambulance driver who has an affair with the nurse, Catherine Barkley, who takes care of him in a hospital in Milan. In the novel, she gets pregnant with his child and dies in childbirth. When asked by one of Hemingway's biographers about the similarities between herself and Barkley, Agnes was cross about the insinuation that she'd had a physical relationship with Hemingway: "I wasn't that kind of girl," she insisted.

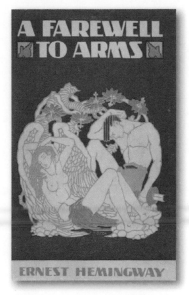

Agnes's relationship with the Italian aristocrat didn't work out because his parents were opposed to it. She continued to work for the Red Cross after the war, in Romania, New York, and then Haiti. While in Haiti, in November 1928, she married a man called Howard Preston Gardiner, a civilian member of the US occupation forces. The marriage failed and she traveled to Reno for a divorce, then in 1934 she married William Stanfield, a widower with three children who lived in New York. They moved to Key West and she visited Cuba several times in the 1940s and 1950s while Hemingway was resident there, but decided not to look him up because she'd heard he was drinking heavily.

Hemingway married four times altogether and became one of the 20th century's most admired novelists, winning the Nobel Prize for Literature in 1954. Agnes had predicted back in 1919: "I somehow feel that some day I'll have reason to be proud of you." But throughout his life he struggled with severe depression, and in 1961 he committed suicide by putting a shotgun in his mouth and pulling the trigger.

Some biographers speculate that Hemingway's rejection by Agnes affected him for the rest of his life, making him leave women before they had a chance to leave him. She certainly broke his heart at a very impressionable age and that seems to have left its mark, making him cynical before his time. "You make love to a girl and then you go away," he told a friend. "She needs someone to make love to her. If the right person turns up, you're out of luck."

"It was just a flirtation," Agnes insisted at the end of her life, when Hemingway was long gone. She'd liked him, but at nineteen he was too immature for a girl who was seven years his senior.

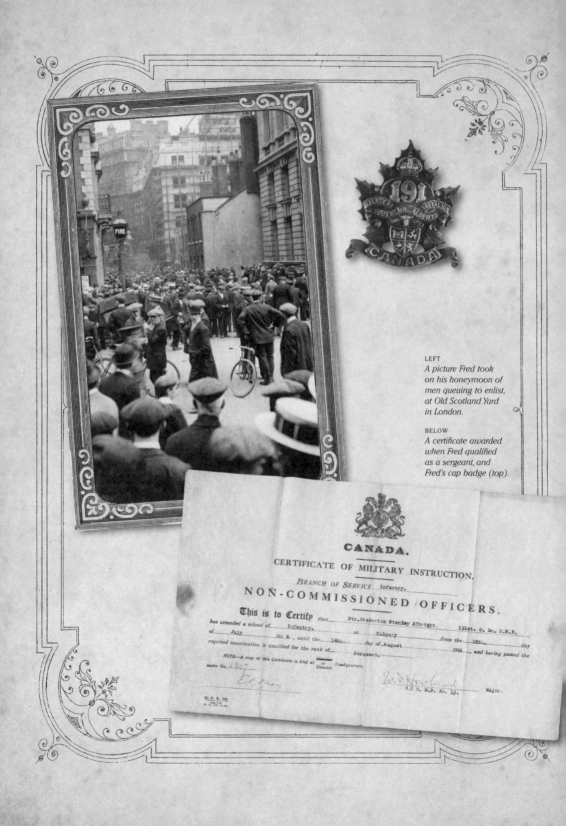

LEFT
A picture Fred took on his honeymoon of men queuing to enlist, at Old Scotland Yard in London.

BELOW
A certificate awarded when Fred qualified as a sergeant, and Fred's cap badge (top).

CANADA.

CERTIFICATE OF MILITARY INSTRUCTION.

BRANCH OF SERVICE Infantry.

NON-COMMISSIONED OFFICERS.

This is to Certify that Pte.Frederick Stanley Albright. 191st. O. Bn. C.E.F.

has attended a school of Infantry, at Calgary from the 12th day

of July 191 6 , until the 14th day of August 1916 , and having passed the

required examination is qualified for the rank of Sergeant.

NOTE—A copy of this Certificate is filed at or District Headquarters.

under No. 6207

G.S.O. M.D. No. 13. Major.

M. F. B. 123.

Fred & Evelyn
ALBRIGHT

Married: June 12, 1914

Frederick Stanley Albright
CANADIAN

—

Born: March 23, 1883

—

Rank & regiment:
Private, 21st Reserve Battalion
Canadian Expeditionary Force

Elnora Evelyn Kelly
CANADIAN

—

Born: November 14, 1890

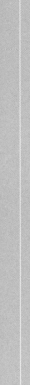

Fred Albright: When Evelyn accused him of being reserved, he replied, "I have always felt that I'd prefer to have my real inmost self unknown to the world and to everybody except one woman."

Evelyn Kelly: She wrote to Fred, "One thing I don't like about being married is that I'll have to take your name, and I like my own better."

FRED AND EVELYN ENJOYED A WONDERFUL HONEYMOON TRAVELING
ROUND BRITAIN, BUT SHE WOKE UP CRYING IN THEIR LONDON
HOTEL ON THE NIGHT OF AUGUST 1, 1914, WITH A FEELING THAT
SOMETHING TERRIBLE WAS ABOUT TO HAPPEN.

F red and Evelyn's family were friends and may have been distantly related, so they grew up knowing each other. In 1903, when Evelyn was just thirteen years old, Fred spent Christmas Day with her family and he gave her "a big apple and some silly verses." He often helped her with her school lessons and when in 1910 he moved from their hometown of Cayuga, Ontario, to Alberta to finish his law degree, they began to write to each other from time to time. She was studying English and History at Victoria College in Ontario when they began the correspondence, in which they discussed politics, literature, religion, women's suffrage, temperance—of which they were both proponents—and all the big issues of the day. The letters were intelligent, often funny, and beautifully written, and gradually they became warmer and more frequent.

When Fred returned to Ontario for a holiday in August 1913, he at last told Evelyn that he had been in love with her since they were youngsters and asked for her hand in marriage. She admitted she had always loved him too and they became engaged, agreeing to wed the following summer. Fred returned to Calgary, where he was now practicing as a lawyer while also lecturing in law at the University of Alberta, and his next letter to Evelyn was a self-conscious love letter. He admitted that his "habit of reserve is not easily broken" but said that he longed to see her and kiss her again. She wrote back teasing that he had to be her "fellow" for a while: "All the girls here have their beaus handy. But you, I have had you two or three weeks, and then I'm going to marry you."

In the letters they analyze when their feelings for each other started and he admits that he had hesitated to declare his because although he had always loved her, he was not sure if they were physically compatible—perhaps because she was very short and slight—but then he realized that true love "is a union of personalities, mind, soul and body."

> ... true love
> "is a union of
> personalities,
> mind, soul
> and body."

ABOVE
Fred and Evelyn's wedding on June 12, 1914, at Thorold Church, Ontario. It was a perfect day, followed by a glorious honeymoon that ended prematurely when war was declared.

OPPOSITE
A telegram from Fred sent on March 25, 1917, as his ship was about to set sail from Halifax bound for England.

Another man, John, had been courting her, but Evelyn explained he didn't "measure up to the standards I had set in my mind, which I knew you fitted." They sometimes quarreled as they negotiated the terms of their future together, but they saw eye to eye on all the major issues, such as woman's suffrage, and both supported a women's right to work after marriage. They even wrote advising each other of the nightwear they would bring for their wedding night!

Fred and Evelyn got married on June 12, 1914, in Thorold, Ontario, and set off on an extended honeymoon starting at Niagara Falls, followed by New York, Ireland, and Great Britain. They had read in the newspapers about the mounting tension in Europe but both were eager to see Britain and didn't think it would come to war. However, when they arrived in London, he wrote in his diary that they "heard the beat of drums and knew troops were marching along the Strand." The Archbishop of Canterbury gave a sermon appealing to all that was "best and noblest in British character," and Fred noted: "Vicissitudes may come and defeats may be ours, but in the end we shall win because the cause is right." They were loyal subjects of the British Empire and listened gravely when war was declared on August 4, three days after Evelyn woke up crying with a feeling of all-pervasive dread.

The War Years

As soon as they could get a passage, Fred and Evelyn sailed back to Canada and set up home in Calgary near his law firm, Clarke, Carlson, and Company. She had already explained that she did not want to rush into starting a family right away: "Of course, I want children, but I don't want them to start on. And you said you didn't either." She enjoyed going to the opera and theater and concerts, and, unusually for a married woman in that era, began working as a trainee at Fred's law firm.

In the summer of 1915, her sister Ora's husband, Art, went to Europe as a medical officer and in October, while Evelyn was back east visiting her family for a few months, Fred signed up for a local militia regiment, the 103rd. He didn't volunteer for active service; he would merely train with the militia so as to be ready if the day came when he was needed, explaining his reasons to Evelyn in a letter: "I have had a terrible battle to fight—to decide how far family ties should be considered in the face of such a pressing and universal need."

It was June 1916 when Fred enlisted as a private in a reserve battalion. As part of the empire, Canadians were fiercely patriotic to Great Britain, and he felt it was his duty. Had he volunteered for the University Battalion, he might have got a commission as an officer, but he chose the 21st Reserve Battalion in the hope that it would allow him to spend as long as possible at home with his wife. Evelyn did not attempt to discourage him from signing up except once when she asked, "Why should we if others do not?" He replied, "Why should others and not we?"

"I have had a terrible battle to fight ..."

During the winter of 1916–17 he worked as a recruiting sergeant in Alberta, and it wasn't until March 3, 1917, that

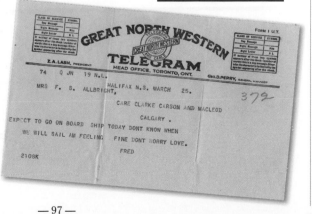

TOP & ABOVE
Bramshott Camp,
Hampshire, summer 1917.
Fred enjoyed his time
cycling around exploring
the English countryside,
but disapproved of the
drunken behavior he
witnessed: "The waste
and squalor and disease
and poverty caused by
drinking is alarming."

he was sent to England to train with the Canadian Overseas Expeditionary Force. He and Evelyn resumed their habit of writing to each other, but her first letters are gloomy as she considers how long it might be before she will see him again: "It is maybe wrong of me to let you know how absolutely I miss you, but that is the chief thing in my life." She was short of money, but focused on studying for her law exams and making up boxes of essentials to mail to her husband in the UK.

During the spring and summer of 1917, Fred was training at Bramshott Camp in Hampshire, England, and enjoyed cycling around country lanes and exploring stately homes during his time off. He wrote to Evelyn about the air raids taking place—"The boom from the guns and dropping bombs became louder and louder . . . we tried to count the planes and I'm sure I counted 36"—and he wrote in his diary about everyday life, commenting that food left on plates was scraped up and reused in soups, stews, or puddings. Evelyn worried that he would be too cold in England and sent him bed socks, but in fact there was hot sun and a muggy atmosphere that left him sweating after each drill. As their third wedding anniversary came and went, Fred recalled what they had been doing on each day of their honeymoon, and he often wrote to Evelyn about how much he loved her: "The glorious thing is that we do love each other now so dearly—yes—and I believe wisely."

Evelyn went back to Ontario for a summer break and suffered a hemorrhage of the uterus, which meant prolonging her stay while she recovered. On her return she went back to work with Fred's law firm and wrote to tell him, jokingly, how "several have said that I was doing your work."

And then, on September 15, Fred wrote with the news that both had been dreading—he was being sent to France—although he hastened to reassure Evelyn that it was bound to be some time before he was sent to the Front. Deep down, with all the talk of a "big push" due to take place that autumn, he probably suspected he would be in the trenches before long, but he didn't want to alarm her. Before leaving, he arranged to have an album of photographs sent back to Evelyn in Canada, hoping it would arrive in good time for her birthday in November.

The Battle of Passchendaele

Fred's descriptive letters to Evelyn continued after they arrived in France on September 17, 1917. He wrote about local vendors crying, "Apools, chocolates!" and described the way they used a mixture of currencies so that a bar of chocolate cost "one franc 4 penny." Much sooner than he had hoped, his company were sent to the trenches, and he wrote on September 28, "For the past week I have washed, shaved & bathed out of

ZEPPELINS

Zeppelin airships had first been developed in the 1890s, and during the war German commanders used them to launch bombing raids on Britain. The airships had a rigid frame of rings and girders containing hydrogen-filled gasbags, with motors underneath to move them and a basket for the navigators to sit in. The first bombing raid of the war hit the Norfolk coast in January 1915 and raids continued until May 1918, causing substantial damage and civilian loss of life. The British army introduced searchlights and anti-aircraft guns, but it proved difficult to puncture the multiple layers of the Zeppelin in order to ignite the hydrogen. On the night of September 2, 1916, the first Zeppelin was shot down by Lt. William Leefe Robinson, who fired three drums' worth of incendiary bullets into the airship SL11, causing it to catch fire, and became a national hero. During the summer of 1917, Fred Albright witnessed several alarming Zeppelin attacks, writing on July 7, "It is reported that the London Genl. Post Office is in flames—that St. Paul's cathedral was also bombed."

LEFT
A recruitment poster with an image of searchlights picking out a Zeppelin in the skies above London.

On Active Service

WITH THE BRITISH
EXPEDITIONARY FORCE

Y.M.C.A.   Y.M.C.A.

Somewhere in France. Sept. 12/17

My dearest,—

This is Wednesday evening and I haven't written you since last Friday before leaving Bramshott. Since then so much has happened and the hours have been so full I haven't even written a word in my diary. I am sorry that the censorship doesn't allow me to give names of places nor any military information, but as I said before you are not to worry about me and always consider no news as good news.

Well we fell in at 8⁰ last Friday night on our battalion parade ground for inspection. Despite the fact that many of the fellows were "broke" they had managed to get some beer and other things to make them happy and lively,—a few even being fairly well "tanked". Of course practically all of the battalion came to see us off. After waiting around for nearly an hour we marched to the brigade parade ground where we were joined by drafts from the other battalions in our brigade. Here we had another wait of more than an hour. Douglas & Herb came to say goodbye and Herb insisted on giving me something. I assured him I had all I needed but he finally went to the Y.M.C.A. & came back with 3 candles and a cake of maple sugar. I really had my pockets all full and thought the candles unnecessary but I took them—and

a shell hole." As a lawyer, a man of erudition, it was not what he was used to. He described the way the men kept very still when German planes flew overhead because "the least movement on the ground is discernible . . . we don't want Heine [the Germans] to know what positions we occupy." He watched a German plane being shot down and all his fellow soldiers gave a cheer.

On the morning of October 20, Fred wrote telling Evelyn that it was "a fair morning again and the sun is shining," then added, "Tell Mrs B. that I am carrying her Belgian coin for luck." (Mrs Brown was a family friend who had given him the coin before he left.) It seems he knew he was being sent to the front line near Ypres that day, where the Third Battle of Ypres (also known as the Battle of Passchendaele) was raging. The village of Passchendaele had been chosen as a target because it was on the supply route for the German Fourth Army, but conditions were atrocious after weeks of heavy rainfall had turned the ground into slippery mud. It was Fred's first engagement in the fighting and it would be his last. On October 26, when Canadian forces joined the battle for the first time, Fred's company was stationed in a badly exposed spot, with no adequate trenches. Fighting was fierce and during the day Fred's position was hit by a shell that killed several men, including him. Only two or three men from his platoon of fifty-two soldiers survived.

BELOW
Fred Albright's grave in Larch Wood cemetery, Zillebeke, near Ypres, Belgium. He had only been in France for six weeks when he was killed.

Unaware of his fate, Evelyn continued to write: "That last winter was very precious," she wrote on October 28. "I think we grew nearer than ever then." On his return she wanted them to move into a new house and "start anew," like being married all over again, "only we shall have all our love and understanding to make things run smoothly." Two weeks later, on November 12, she received the dreaded telegram: "Deeply regret inform you 895173 Pte. Frederick Stanley Albright was officially reported killed in action."

Fred was buried at Larch Wood Cemetery near Ypres. On November 6, Canadian troops finally succeeded in taking the small village of Passchendaele but at huge cost to both sides.

THE EFFECTS OF SHELLING

In September 1914, at the Battle of the Marne, a group of soldiers were found standing dead at their posts without any obvious injuries. A rumor spread that the huge new field guns being used could cause dark forces to move through the air and damage men's brains. Some who survived heavy shelling turned up at casualty clearing stations badly confused and trembling, with headaches, dizziness, and memory loss, and medics at first diagnosed these cases as physical injuries caused by trauma to the brain from an explosion. However, many commanders believed "shell shock" to be a nervous complaint, a kind of emotional collapse that occurred in men who hadn't necessarily been exposed to shelling, and so the debate began: was it physical or mental? At the end of the war a British government report on shell shock stated that only a small proportion of cases (5 to 10 percent) had physical concussion following shelling and that the rest were of nervous disposition. An estimated 1,663,445 men (10 percent of all those wounded in the war) were diagnosed as suffering from shell shock. But Fred Albright was killed by shell concussion, when the blast waves from a shell did indeed cause fatal damage to his brain without producing any external sign of injury, just like those men at the Marne.

ABOVE
A shell exploding during the Battle of Passchendaele: A Red Cross volunteer described being caught in the blast force as "like being struck unexpectedly by a huge wave in the ocean."

Almost 16,000 Canadians were killed for a victory that ultimately had little strategic value.

Struggling with the enormity of her grief, Evelyn carried on writing to Fred in a notebook, letters that would never be sent: "I suppose it seems silly to write to you, but . . . I go on pretending as I have ever since you went away last March, that you were coming home again . . . I shall try to live cheerfully and well, but it seems that I am like a tree, half killed by my [sic] lightning." She spent hours poring over the book of photographs, the last gift he had sent her. As Christmas approached, she wrote about that other Christmas fourteen years before when he gave her an apple and some silly verses. She wrote to him about the details of her day-to-day life— "Today I have been re-lining my coat"— still sharing them as they had when he was alive. She wrote of friends who were being kind, of books she was reading. And she wrote how bitterly she regretted not having had a child with him: "Oh dearest, if I had only someone who looked like you, who was part of you, to love."

Evelyn bravely continued with her law studies and graduated as a lawyer in 1919, coming third in the province. After that, she returned to Ontario to live with her father and joined the English department at the University of Western Ontario. By 1934 she had been promoted to Associate Professor, specializing in 18th-century English literature. She never remarried. She had already met her great love, and their two years, nine months of domestic bliss, as well as the 550 letters they had written to each other over a fourteen-year relationship, provided her with enough loving memories to last a lifetime.

> *"Oh dearest, if I had only someone who looked like you, who was part of you, to love."*

ABOVE
When Evelyn graduated in 1919, she became only the second woman to qualify as a lawyer in the province of Alberta.

BELOW
*The Queen's Own Cameron
Highlanders, who fought in Highland
dress. Out of thirteen battalions of
just over a thousand men each, they
lost 5,930 men during the war and
gained fifty-seven honors in battle,
including three Victoria Crosses.*

THE QUEEN'S OWN,
CAMERON HIGHLANDERS.

A Charge up the hill.

Harry Payne

Hugh & Jessie
MANN

Married: October 15, 1914

Hugh Wallace Mann
SCOTTISH

Born: January 13, 1891

*Rank & regiment:
Captain, 5th Battalion, The
Queen's Own Cameron
Highlanders*

Jessie Reid
SCOTTISH

Born: July 11, 1895

ABOVE
Hugh as a second lieutenant in 1916.
"I'm just fair longing to see you and
our nipper," he wrote to Jessie, "and if
something doesn't turn up, I'll desert."

AS THE SON OF A MINISTER WHO WAS HIMSELF STUDYING FOR
THE MINISTRY, ONE MIGHT HAVE EXPECTED HUGH TO BE A RATHER
SERIOUS YOUNG MAN, BUT INSTEAD HIS LETTERS TO JESSIE SHOW
HIM TO BE WITTY, IRREVERENT, AND FULL OF FUN.

Hugh attended Glasgow University at the same time as Jessie's brother, Arnold, and the two became close friends. Hugh could either have met Jessie when Arnold invited him to the Reid family home in Glasgow, or they might have bumped into each other for the first time at Hugh's and Arnold's graduation ceremony in June 1911. In an early letter to her in July 1911, Hugh talks of their "ancient friendship," but this could well have been a joke given the light-hearted tone of the rest, in which he teases her about her "deplorable writing."

Jessie was the fourth of seven children and was born in Alva, Clackmannanshire. When the family moved to Glasgow in 1904, she attended the High School for Girls, where teachers commended her as "a pupil of great promise." She was intelligent, with a pretty face and a cheerful smile, and despite her youth Hugh started writing to her when the Reid family went on holiday to the Isle of Arran in the summer of 1911. She replied to his letters, romance blossomed, and by January 1912 the two were already talking of marriage. "I suppose it will be a few years before we set out together, but it will be," he promised. He particularly enjoyed planning where they would take their honeymoon, suggesting various locations for her approval.

Although Hugh called her K, Kid, or Kiddie in his early letters (she was five years his junior), there is no doubting his passion for Jessie: "I want to hold you close and closer, to look into your eyes . . . and to kiss you, Kid, till I have to order your little heart to stop thump-thumping." By the summer of 1913 he was sufficiently welcomed in the Reid family to join them on their holiday in Arran, but had to hurry back to Glasgow after his father took ill and subsequently died. Jessie was Hugh's steady support during this difficult time,

> "I want to hold you close and closer, to look into your eyes ... and to kiss you ... till I have to order your little heart to stop thump-thumping."

and he wrote to her how much he regretted that she never got to meet his father, who would have "rejoiced" in their love.

In autumn 1913 Jessie started her own degree at Glasgow University, studying Latin and Mathematics, while Hugh worked at the Wellpark United Free Church in Greenock, west of Glasgow. Their love deepened during the year and then in summer 1914 came what he referred to obliquely as a "debacle." First of all Jessie began to take "seedy turns" and then it was confirmed that she was expecting a baby. "Keep up your heart, little one," Hugh wrote, the stress obvious in his tone. "I guess it will be alright."

A Wedding and an Enlistment

Hugh's family certainly didn't think news of the pregnancy was "alright." It could ruin his chances of making a career as a minister in the very strict Free Church and bring shame on them all. A hasty registry office wedding took place on October 15, 1914 without guests, who might have spotted Jessie's condition, and on the same day Hugh signed up to fight in the battalion being enlisted by Colonel D.W. Cameron of Lochiel, as advertised on the sides of

LEFT
*Jessie and Micky outside
the schoolhouse in
Ardeonaig when he was
about three months old.
There were just nineteen
pupils in the school.*

buses across Glasgow at the time. Jessie was sent to stay with her
married sister in Sheffield under instruction that she must not set
foot in Glasgow, or even in Edinburgh, lest any family friends see
her condition. There was no question of her continuing her university
degree. Hugh was saddened by the turn of events, wondering when
he could be with Jessie again, but he followed his mother and
uncle's wishes that they keep their marriage secret until such time
as the child could be passed off as one conceived within wedlock.

The baby, officially named Duncan but always referred to by
Hugh and Jessie as "Micky," was born in January 1915. Still the
argument raged about where Jessie should live until finally her
mother became angry about what she called her daughter's
"persecution" and took a teaching post in a little village called
Ardeonaig, where her daughter and grandson would live with her
for the next couple of years. The location on Loch Tay was so
remote that it took the best part of a day to reach it from Glasgow,
making it perfect for keeping the child's birth secret, though difficult
for Hugh and Jessie to meet when he got leave from the army.

He started his training in Inverness, then in January 1915 went
south to Aldershot and Cirencester before being sent over to
France in July. Right from the start, Jessie sent regular packages full
of his favorite foods from home: oatcakes and butter, eggs—which
miraculously arrived "fresh as paint"—and biscuits. She also sent
tobacco, although before the war she had frequently nagged him

ABOVE
Hugh with his two-year-old son during a brief period of home leave in September 1917. "Love to my own dear wee sonnie boy," he wrote afterward.

to cut down on his smoking. She got baby Micky to scribble in one letter and Hugh replied, "He's a remarkable writer for his age, ain't he?"

Initially, Hugh's battalion of the Cameron Highlanders were digging trenches, but as early as September 25, 1915, at the Battle of Loos, they saw their first action, about which Hugh wrote home, "Hell can hold no hotter corner. For hours we held that damned line against constant counter attack, and ceaseless enfilade fire, and always one was waiting one's turn to be hit." The Scotsmen acquitted themselves admirably, securing the town of Loos and a hill known as Hill 70, though at great cost: 6,500 men died from the 15th Scottish Division, with Hugh being the only sergeant left in his company. In his battalion there were 75 percent casualties: he had lost almost all his army friends while, he wrote, "All I got was a bullet thro' my sleeve and a bit of shrapnel ripping my hose-top." (Hugh wore a kilt and the hose-top was the top of his socks, which were folded double just below the knee.)

That autumn, Hugh was sent home to Scotland on sick leave with a nasty case of recurring boils, which he described as "an ideal malady for a person of my sunny disposition" because "they don't give me the least pain." He was tasked with drafting new recruits over the course of 1916 and he also did some preaching with the United Free Church, but best of all he was able to spend time with Jessie and their son. Gradually, they were letting people know about their marriage and parenthood, and even visited her sister in Bristol together in October 1916. Hugh could have seen out the rest of the war from Scotland, but he complained of feeling "tame-catty" (cowardly) and anxious to get back to the Front to do his bit. Despite his love for Jessie—"I take spells of desperate longing to see you, Jess, and hold you in my arms and kiss you till you cry for mercy"—he pushed for a commission to return to France, and it came through in late 1916 when he learned he would be joining the 5th Battalion of the Cameron Highlanders. In February 1917, he was once more back at the Western Front.

From Arras to Passchendaele

Hugh soon got back into the rhythm of time in the trenches under heavy shellfire followed by rest periods behind the lines. He wrote about taking part in a game of bridge one afternoon when suddenly a shell came through their billet, commenting wryly that "somehow the game lost its interest after that." In April, his battalion got through the Battle of Arras with only 85 losses, but with typical understatement, he described France as "an entirely unhealthy residential area." He took a course to learn about the new Lewis gun, a machine gun developed in the US, and

LIFE AT THE FRONT

Troops were sent to the front line in rotation, so most men spent just four to six days firing and being fired upon before they were sent back behind the lines for a period of "rest" (which in practice might mean road building or other manual work). Hugh complained bitterly when his unit was stuck at the Front for eight days because someone forgot to relieve them. Sleep was difficult in the trenches due to the noise and discomfort, and water for washing was in short supply. There was usually a metal brazier supplying heat and a bucket or nearby shell hole served as a toilet. Rations were barely edible by the time they reached the men and the British complained bitterly about the tins of "bully beef" that were their standard fare, preferring "Maconochie's," a mixture of meat and root vegetables. When they ventured across no-man's-land during offensives, they found that German trenches tended to be dug deeper and had more home comforts than the British and French ones.

BELOW
Sandbags and planks shore up the earth in this basic trench, c. 1916.

ABOVE
Two soldiers of the Cameron Highlanders using a Maxim gun, a new type of machine gun.

in June was promoted to commander of his company, an honor he glossed over in his letters. As summer progressed, depression took hold of him and he admitted to Jessie that he had "several times resigned myself to a crown and a harp at the *toute de suite*" (in other words, to death).

In September 1917, Hugh's spirits were lifted immeasurably by a brief period of home leave, which he described as a time of "infinite tenderness" and "just like a bit of heaven all the time." Jessie replied: "I'm glad it was so happy for you, dear, for that is what I wanted it to be . . . and you are to have a whole long lifetime of it."

When Hugh got back across the Channel, his battalion had moved into Belgium, near Ypres, where the ground was waterlogged by heavy rain. "This kind of thing makes moving about in the bogs and shell-holes ... vastly unpleasant," he commented. His battalion was to be part of a big Allied push in this region and he seemed to have a sense of foreboding when he wrote of the "howling gale with lashing unceasing rain." On the night of October 12, as part of the Battle of Passchendaele, his men went over the top into no-man's-land and in the chaos of battle Hugh was wounded in the left thigh. He was carried from the field and two days later was taken by train to a hospital in Le Tréport on the Normandy coast.

Unaware of Hugh's injury, Jessie kept writing to him regularly until October 18, when she received a telegram from the War Office informing her that he had "gunshot wound left thigh severe," followed by a letter from him in which he makes light of the injury. However, she soon realized it could be more serious than he was letting on and traveled across to Le Tréport to be with him, leaving Micky in Ardeonaig with her mother. She found Hugh delirious with fever in his hospital bed and needing morphine in order to sleep. He had difficulty eating and soon grew very weak, but she wrote optimistically to her mother that he was "fighting well" and that "every day that passes will bring him nearer safety."

But it was not to be. On November 12, Hugh died, probably as a result of gas gangrene, a deadly form of gangrene that causes gas to be produced in infected tissues. Jessie was by his side right until the end, and she was there when he was buried in a military cemetery near the hospital with a wooden cross to mark his grave. One of the nurses who had tended him was distraught and wrote to Jessie that in ten years of nursing, "Never have I been more grieved and sadder than I am now about your own dear boy." Her father wrote, "Our hearts are sore for you my dear in your great grief, but you will have the memory with you always that

> " *... several times I have resigned myself to a crown and a harp at the toute de suite ...* "

BELOW
The Battle of Passchendaele, or Third Battle of Ypres, from July 31 to November 10, 1917, cost both sides dearly and served no real tactical purpose. Here stretcher-bearers struggle in the deep mud.

MEDICAL FACILITIES IN FRANCE

Medics at regimental aid posts just behind the front line could perform first aid, but the seriously wounded had to be taken by field ambulance to a casualty clearing station, normally about 9 miles behind the lines. There patients were assessed in a reception area, and those who were severely wounded and suffering from shock were treated in a resuscitation area, where they were placed in heated beds and given blood transfusions to prepare them for surgery. It was found that the best way to prevent fatal infections and gas gangrene in wounds was cutting out all dead and injured tissue within 36 hours, but this was not always possible. The bacilli that caused gangrene were pervasive in the muddy soil and on the shell fragments within wounds, and could proliferate even after amputation of the affected limb. Patients who required longer-term care were sent to general hospitals that were also accessible on the French railway network, such as the one in Le Tréport where Hugh was treated. If they'd got a "blighty" (the colloquial term for a wound that earned them a period of recuperative leave at home), soldiers would be shipped back to a military hospital in the UK as soon as they were well enough to travel.

RIGHT
The telegram officially informing Jessie of Hugh's death.

your dear one did his duty nobly and died a hero's death." When Jessie got back to Scotland she was given a package of the last eight letters she had written to him marked "undelivered," along with some of his personal possessions, including a tiny suede wallet in which he had kept a photograph of her and his son at Ardeonaig.

Jessie's mother brought little Micky, who was now almost three years old, back to Glasgow where he would be Jessie's "comfort and her shield" in the coming years, while she was still in deep mourning for the loss of the love of her life. The young boy flourished at school and was on track for a great future, but then the unthinkable happened when in 1931 he died at the age of sixteen after a short illness. Jessie never remarried but moved in with her sister, Dine, and devoted her life to working for the church and sometimes helping out in the school.

Though Jessie and Hugh had only had a relatively short time as husband

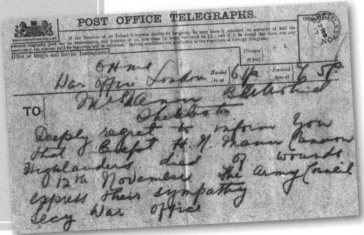

and wife, their love was deep and she must have taken comfort during her grief in all the wonderful love letters Hugh had written her between July 10, 1911 and October 19, 1917. In an early one he wrote, "I wish you could hand over your toothache to me. I would positively enjoy having it, if I knew it would save you pain." In that last letter, as he lay in his hospital bed seriously wounded, he concluded, "This morning the world looks very beautiful, and full of joy to me … All my love, precious, to you and my darling boy. Yours, Hugh."

> *"All my love, precious, to you and my darling boy."*

ABOVE
*Percy received an ANZAC
Gallipoli medallion, issued
to all the Australian and
New Zealand troops who
served there between
the landing in April 1915
and the evacuation in
January 1916.*

"The Australian and New Zealand troops have indeed
proved themselves worthy sons of the Empire."
GEORGE R.I.

Percy & Dorothy SMYTHE

Married: June 7, 1919

Percy Ellesmere Smythe
AUSTRALIAN
—
February 5, 1893
—
Rank & regiment:
Lieutenant, 24th Battalion
Australian Imperial Forces

Dorothy Nellie Jewell
BRITISH
—
September 18, 1899

ABOVE
*The Smythe brothers, from left to right: Vern,
Bert, Percy, and Viv. All four would serve but
only three would return.*

PERCY DECIDED HE WANTED TO MARRY DOROTHY WITHIN THREE WEEKS OF THEIR FIRST MEETING, BUT THEY FACED STRONG OPPOSITION FROM HER FAMILY, WHO WERE DETERMINED TO STOP HER FROM EMIGRATING TO THE OTHER SIDE OF THE WORLD.

Percy grew up in a large family of one older brother, three sisters, and four younger brothers, in the little outback town of Jerilderie, New South Wales, Australia, where their father worked as a bootmaker. Money was tight, so the boys left school early to work but continued to take lessons from their grandfather in the evenings. Percy enjoyed sketching and writing and in April 1906, at the age of thirteen, he won a silver medal for one of his poems. When war was declared in 1914, the four oldest boys all enlisted in the Australian Imperial Forces. Percy was turned down at first because his chest measurement was an inch and a half too small (34 inches was the minimum). Then he saw an ad in the paper for Snowy Baker's Physical Culture School and within a week the exercises they prescribed had increased his chest to the requisite size, enabling him to enlist and begin his training in May 1915.

His brothers, Bert and Vern, were present at the landing of Australian troops in Gallipoli, but Percy didn't set sail till July. His mother came to see him off and he shed a few tears as the ship

BELOW
ANZAC troops landed on the Gallipoli peninsula to try to drive out Turkish troops guarding the Dardanelles straits, but the resistance was too strong and they failed to break out of their beachheads.

pulled away, wondering whether all of his brothers would return safely. His company sailed up the Suez Canal and stopped in Gallipoli, where he had his first taste of life in the firing line "Lying there with my head to the ground it sounded for all the world like a saucepan-full of porridge boiling very quickly," he wrote in the diary he would keep throughout the war years. Conditions were poor, with decaying corpses left on the ground and maggots crawling everywhere, and he soon succumbed to pneumonia, which had him laid up in a Maltese hospital for three months to regain his strength. By 1916, he was back on duty in Egypt and then Northern France, and he whiled away the time in the trenches writing stories, which he sent off to magazines and literary agencies (with no immediate success), and drawing sketches of the scenes around him. In July, he was caught up in the fierce battle at Pozières, when Australian forces captured a crucial ridge but suffered heavy losses in the process. He was buried in a dugout after one round of heavy shelling and had to be rescued by comrades.

BELOW
Percy's drawing at Corbie Abbey in Picardy, France, from August 1915. He enjoyed sketching churches, gardens, and battlefield scenes.

On Christmas Eve 1916, his chest still weak, Percy caught bronchitis and was sent to England to recuperate. He was still there in May 1917 when he got word that his older brother Bert had been killed in the trenches east of Bullecourt. His strong religious faith helped him to accept it as God's will, but he was still moved to tears a couple of weeks later when the mail brought him a letter from Bert with a gift of seven shillings "in case he was short."

On August 23, 1917, Percy met a girl named Dorothy Jewell while waiting at a train station in Birmingham and they fell into conversation. She told him she worked for the Canteen Board at Ludgershall, providing meals for servicemen, and before she left he had persuaded her to go on a date with him three days later. In his diary, he described her as "a bonnie little lass, lively and innocent"—but it didn't stop him going out on a date with someone else the next day. It seems Percy had always had an eye for the ladies. He was in correspondence with some girls in Australia who seemed interested in him; there was also a nurse in the hospital in Malta who had taken a liking to him; plus a couple of "delightful young flappers" in France; and not forgetting at least two other girls he'd kissed while in Birmingham. But Dorothy was different—"roguish, loving and lovable" —and within three weeks of meeting her Percy had decided he was going to propose. It wasn't quite love at first sight, but it wasn't far off.

The Jewell Family

Dorothy's father was very strict and, rather than sneak around behind his back, Percy approached him directly and asked permission to go out with his daughter. To his surprise, the answer was a firm no. Mr Jewell said that at seventeen she was too young and, anyway, she was already corresponding with another soldier by the name of

CONSCIENTIOUS OBJECTORS

One of Percy's religious friends, Jack Elliott, was fiercely opposed to the war, claiming that it was at odds with Christian values, but Percy wrote, "He only sees the wickedness of all this slaughter, without considering all the righteous self-sacrifice and suffering that has taken place." Those who refused to fight because of their beliefs were known as conscientious objectors or "conchies." Some objected on political grounds, arguing that Germany was not the enemy and that there were different ways to solve the problems between the countries; for Quakers and Jehovah's Witnesses, war was against their religion; and pacifists were against war in general. After the draft was introduced, in most countries conscientious objectors had to appear before tribunals explaining their reasons for refusing to fight, and they were frequently ordered to do war work on the home front or behind the lines; those who refused might be jailed. Public opinion was strongly against conchies; they were often handed white feathers—symbolizing cowardice—when out in public.

George Pike. Percy was undeterred—he wrote in his diary that she was "a dear little girl, with auburn hair and grey eyes full of mirth" —and Dorothy liked him enough to risk her father's wrath. Together they managed to escape his watchful eye and go for long walks or bicycle rides in the countryside, or attend church together, where Percy was delighted to hear that she had a pretty singing voice. On September 15, they had a frivolous conversation in which Dorothy declared that she would not get married before the age of 25, while Percy tried to persuade her that 19 was a better age. They tossed a coin—"two heads for 23, two tails for 19, and one of each for 21, and 21 won the toss." But there were still two obstacles in their way: her father and the war.

In October 1917 Percy was sent back out to the front line, and had a narrow escape when his trench was gassed and the tapes of his respirator became twisted. He got a lungful of poison gas before managing to get his mask on and was shocked to see that a shell had landed just two feet from his head. Letters from Dorothy provided consolation in the midst of hardship. She sent him a New Testament and a pocket wallet containing her photograph, as well as the reassurance that she had written to George Pike to tell him she could no longer be his girl, news it seems that left him deeply upset.

At the end of November, Percy was back in England on leave and spending a musical evening with Dorothy, her mother, and some friends, when her father came home unexpectedly. He was furious to discover that Percy had continued to see his daughter

> ... she was "a dear little girl, with auburn hair and grey eyes full of mirth ..."

after he had forbidden it and was abrupt with them both. The next day Percy wrote to him, formally asking permission to get engaged to Dorothy. In a man-to-man conversation, Mr Jewell explained that he didn't have a high opinion of Australians in general, that he and his wife knew nothing about Percy or his family but had to take them "on trust," and that he certainly wouldn't consent to Dorothy marrying and going off to live in Australia after the war. She was

needed at home to help look after her younger brother and sister, Wilf and Betty. Dorothy was distressed by his views, but declared to Percy she would marry him regardless. They settled on the date of June 1919, eighteen months later, by which time she hoped to have won her father over to the idea.

Percy went back to the Front, but there was a slight hiccup in the courtship at this point when Dorothy found out that he had been seen with another girl while at officer training school in Cambridge. Percy hurriedly wrote to Dorothy with an innocent explanation and she claimed she forgave him, but in a letter soon afterward she described going out dancing—an obvious ploy to make him jealous which seems to have worked well. Meanwhile, Dorothy's mother suggested a solution to the problem of her father's objection to their engagement—get married but agree to live in England after the war. Percy explained to Dorothy he couldn't do this as he had already promised his mother faithfully that he would come home.

Before long he was sent back into the heat of battle. In August 1918, his men were commanded to take over some German trenches during the Battle of Dompierre and they captured several prisoners. Percy asked his comrade not to shoot a wounded "Hun" who "tried to hold up his hands, the look on his face a piteous plea for mercy" but the man fired all the same. At the end of the month,

BELOW
Australian troops in the attack on Mont Saint-Quentin at which Percy earned a Military Cross for helping to rescue the wounded.

they crossed the Somme to Mont Saint-Quentin, where he helped
dozens of men wounded after shelling there. "Dead, wounded,
and dying, all lay twisted and huddled together in grotesque little
heaps, a mass of mangled flesh," he wrote in his diary. The next
day he got some shrapnel embedded in his cheek, but a minor
scratch did not warrant leaving the battlefield. This was the scene
of what British commander General Sir Henry Rawlinson described
as "the greatest military achievement of the war," when the
Australian 21st, 23rd and 24th Battalions stormed the village of
Mont Saint-Quentin and captured the hill site, with Percy among
them. The Germans were pushed back to the Hindenburg Line,
their position of the previous spring, and 2,600 German prisoners
were taken. When the five days of solid fighting were over, Percy
collapsed from exhaustion and was taken to a casualty clearing
station to recover. At the end of October he heard that he was to
be awarded a Military Cross for his actions at Mont Saint-Quentin.

Shortly afterward, on November 11, 1918, Armistice was declared.
Percy and two of his brothers had survived the war, but he was
determined not to return to Australia without Dorothy by his side,
so there was one last battle he had to fight.

ABOVE
*German prisoners of
war captured by the
Australians on August 8,
1918, after the Battle
of Dompierre.*

SPANISH INFLUENZA

Percy had a narrow escape from the deadly flu pandemic that swept the globe between 1918 and 1920 after he was billeted in February 1919 with a Belgian man who fell ill and died of influenza in the next room. Unlike normal winter flu, this virus seemed to attack and kill the fit and healthy rather than the weak, as it caused a fatal overreaction of the immune system in which the body started attacking its own cells. It spread quickly through troops in confined areas, such as in the trenches, in military camps, or on board ships, with roughly 50 percent of those who came into contact with the virus catching it. It also crossed continents with the movements of armies. The governments of countries at war tried to keep the facts from the media to avoid creating panic, but it was widely reported in Spain, which was not at war, giving the false impression that the epidemic was most serious there (thus the name "Spanish influenza"). In fact, 500 million people were infected worldwide, and it's estimated that the flu killed between 50 and 100 million of them—3 to 5 percent of the world's then population. This was far more than the estimated 10 million soldiers and 7 million civilians who died due to the war.

The Cost of a Marriage

Mr. and Mrs. Jewell did all they could to prevent Dorothy and Percy from marrying. Mrs. Jewell argued that Dorothy's health was too precarious for marriage since she suffered from rheumatism. Mr. Jewell asked why they couldn't wait for a couple of years and declared that once she got to Australia, Dorothy would be so homesick she would turn around and come home again. Undeterred, Percy and Dorothy decided that if they did not have her parents' permission, they would travel to Scotland, where the age of consent was lower, and marry there instead. Right up until the last moment, they hoped her parents would relent and let the marriage take place in her hometown, but it wasn't to be.

On May 23, 1919, they traveled to Glasgow, where Dorothy stayed with a minister for the requisite fifteen days of residency that made them eligible for a marriage license, and on June 7 they got married in a brief, solemn ceremony. They honeymooned at Balloch on the banks of Loch Lomond and had a wonderful time rowing on the loch and going for walks along the shore.

ABOVE
Stretcher-bearers wear masks to avoid catching the highly contagious influenza virus in October, 1918.

Percy and Dorothy made one last visit to her parents, this time as a married couple, but the meeting was strained. On August 23, when they set sail for Australia, neither Mr. nor Mrs. Jewell came to see them off.

They had struggled long and hard to be together ...

Bad news awaited Percy on arrival in Australia six weeks later: his father had been fatally injured when he was run over by an ambulance after stepping off a trolley. Percy and Dorothy traveled to Sydney to live with his grieving mother but, as her parents had predicted, she was fiercely homesick, especially after she gave birth to a stillborn child in 1920. Percy suffered from chronic bronchitis caused by his war experiences and he tried farming for a couple of years, as he felt the outdoor life helped his chest. The couple had a daughter, Betty, in 1923 and Dorothy gradually began to enjoy her Australian lifestyle, caring for her daughter, cooking for her family and friends, playing the piano, and singing. Dorothy took Betty back to England for a visit when she was three years old, hoping for a family reconciliation, but found that, although pleased to see her, her father had still not forgiven her for emigrating. Meanwhile, Percy still wanted to become a writer, so he worked hard to get himself a place at a university, the first member of his family to achieve such a thing. He became a teacher at a private coaching college and wrote some well-regarded study guides, as well as poems, stories, and a one-act play that was presented on the radio in 1934.

In 1939, after Dorothy's mother died, her father was lonely and he accepted Percy's offer to pay for him and Dorothy's younger brother and sister, Wilf and Betty, to come to live in Australia. The years had mellowed him and he missed his daughter, so was glad to be near her once more. Percy and Dorothy twice traveled back to Europe themselves: in 1954 and 1961–2. Percy visited the war memorial at Villers-Brettoneux, where Bert's name was engraved on a wall, as well as revisiting the scenes of the battles he had taken part in.

The couple bought a holiday cottage at Paradise Beach in Pittwater, New South Wales, where they entertained regularly, but Dorothy hung onto some English customs, always cooking a full Christmas dinner on December 25, despite the blazing heat outside. They had struggled long and hard to be together but, although she outlived Percy by eighteen years, Dorothy never for one moment regretted the decision she had made when she decided to place her future in his hands and make a life with him in Australia.

ABOVE
A brass box given to 427,000 British forces as a Christmas present in 1914. It was the idea of Princess Mary and contained her photograph along with tobacco, writing materials, or candy.

RIGHT
Joseph's service medals.

Joseph & Mary
HEAPES

Married: August 5, 1919

Joseph Heapes

IRISH

Born: September 20, 1887

*Rank & regiment:
Lance Corporal, 2nd Battalion
Royal Irish Regiment*

Mary Fearon

IRISH

Born: August 16, 1885

ABOVE
Officers of Joseph's regiment, the Royal Irish Rifles, stationed at Belfast, 1914.

Certified that No.8285 L/C Heapes, 1st. Bn. Royal Irish Rifles, was Orderly Corpl. in this Hospital, for about three months and during that period he has done his duties satisfactorily. I can recommend him to anyone requiring a reliable man

EDGMacpherson
Major, R.A.M.C.,
Commanding Station Hospital, Kamptee

STATION HOSPITAL
KAMPTEE

RIGHT
A letter of reference from Joseph's commanding officer in India: "I can recommend him to anyone requiring a reliable man."

MARY STARTED WRITING TO JOSEPH DURING HIS YEARS IN A GERMAN PRISONER-OF-WAR CAMP TO HELP RAISE HIS SPIRITS, BUT WHEN SHE FELL IN LOVE WITH HIM, SHE FACED HOSTILITY FROM HER FRIENDS

A s a boy, Joseph lived with his parents and his seven brothers and sisters in the gate lodge of an estate owned by Captain Robert Henry Fowler in Rahinstown, County Meath, Ireland. Young Joseph was so impressed by Captain Fowler, a distinguished career officer in the British army and a renowned cricket player, that he determined to join the army himself one day. There was little other employment in the area, so in August 1900, at the age of thirteen or fourteen, he ran away from home and made his way to Belfast, where he tried to enlist. The enlisting officer took one look at him, asked a few shrewd questions about his age, and got a policeman to escort him home to his mother. In fact, it wasn't until several years later, when Joseph was eighteen, that he finally managed to enlist in the Royal Irish Rifles.

He had hoped for excitement and adventure, and that's certainly what he got over the next few years. First he was in stationed in Delhi, then in 1909 the company moved to Maymo, Upper Burma, where he served with the mounted infantry; in 1911 he was in Mandalay then in 1912 back in India, where he served as an orderly corporal in the hospital in Kamptee. He became a reservist in 1913, having

BELOW
Joseph was working as a groom when war broke out; this experience would have been useful as horses were vital for transporting guns and equipment behind the lines.

THE CHRISTMAS TRUCE

In the first months of the war, before the gas attacks and slaughter of the Somme, relations between individual Germans and their British counterparts were not as hostile as they would later become. On Christmas Eve 1914, German troops along the northern sector of the Western Front decorated their trenches with candles and Christmas trees, and began singing carols. The British responded by singing their own carols and shouting greetings, and through messengers an unofficial truce was agreed for Christmas Day. Soldiers walked out into no-man's-land and exchanged gifts of tobacco and food with their opposite numbers, some offering small souvenirs such as uniform buttons. It was also an opportunity to collect and bury the dead lying there. In several places, impromptu football matches took place between British and German soldiers. It is estimated that as many as 100,000 French, German, and British soldiers, including Joseph's comrades in the Irish Rifles, took part in this unofficial Christmas Day truce, although this unofficial peace-making was roundly condemned by their superior officers.

completed the time he signed up for, and received glowing references from his superior officers: "I can recommend him to anyone requiring a reliable man," wrote one. "He is a man of exemplary character," wrote another, calling him "steady and hardworking." He took a job as a groom for the Benison family at their estate in Slieve Russell, Ballyconnell, where his responsibilities included looking after the ponies and the cars owned by his employer, Joseph Benison.

However, his days as a groom were not to last. On August 5, 1914, the day after the declaration of war, Joseph was recalled to the army. The 1st Battalion was on service in Aden in the Middle East, so Joseph was attached to the 2nd Battalion and by August 14 was already in Rouen. The British Expeditionary Force of regular soldiers came to around 80,000 men, and the plan was to deploy them on the left flank of the French army around the small town of Maubeuge. The German 1st and 2nd Armies were advancing quickly through Belgium, and it was decided that the BEF would make a stand at the Mons-Condé Canal. At dawn on August 23, the Germans charged on British lines and were astonished by a rapid hail of rifle fire that cut them down in the thousands. They hadn't expected the British to get forces out there so quickly, and the men who took aim that day were all professional, well-trained soldiers. However, by the end of the 23rd the sheer weight of German numbers forced the British to retreat, especially after reports reached them that the French 5th Army was pulling back and they risked being encircled. On the 26th, part of the retreating force made a stand at Le Câtelet and the 2nd Irish Rifles engaged the enemy near Caudry, losing around 60 men, with 34 wounded. But although casualties were higher for the British than for the Germans, the Battle of Le Câtelet was critical in holding back the German advance long enough to give British forces time to regroup.

The retreat continued for over 100 miles south to Aisne, where the BEF halted. The men were exhausted and suffering from severe blisters, and there were intermittent exchanges of fire with the pursuing enemy. On September 15, the 2nd Irish came upon strong German lines right ahead of them and could go no further. There were a number of skirmishes and in a German attack on their line on September 20, Joseph was surrounded and taken prisoner. His war was over.

The German guards treated him well, but Joseph was devastated. All he wanted was to get back to his company, but there was no chance of that as he was loaded onto a train and transported back far behind the front lines. It must have been terrifying, as he spoke no German and had no idea what would happen to him. He was taken to one camp, then another, and in early December 1914 he

Joseph was surrounded and taken prisoner. His war was over.

TOP
A clearly shocked private in the Irish Rifles shortly after being taken prisoner by the Germans.

OPPOSITE
Men who had been shooting each other the day before exchanged gifts on December 25, 1914, as British and German soldiers mingled on the Western Front.

arrived at a place called Limburg where there were many other Irish prisoners-of-war. He was met by a Catholic priest, who reassured him that he was safe and would be well treated. The rooms in which they slept were well ventilated, there were plenty of blankets against the cold, and at first the food wasn't at all bad.

Limburg seemed to Joseph to have a high percentage of Irish prisoners, and on December 17 he realized why when an ex-British diplomat named Roger Casement stood up in front of the men and made a speech trying to recruit them into an Irish Brigade he was forming. His goal was to rise up against the British back in Dublin and fight for home rule for Ireland. Casement said he had secured a guarantee from the Kaiser that Ireland would not be invaded by Germany, and he told the men that if they joined him they would be freed immediately.

According to Private William Dooley of the 2nd Royal Irish, "The men were very restless during the speech but they restrained themselves to the end. Then, as Casement passed by, they let themselves go, hushing, hissing, and calling him all sorts of names." Of around 1,800 Irishmen in Limburg, Casement only raised 56 volunteers for his brigade, and these were immediately whisked away to a fancy hotel in the town.

The Irish commanding officers at Limburg sent a message to the camp commandant saying that they didn't want any special treatment because, "in addition to being Irish Catholics, we have the honor to be British soldiers." After this, conditions deteriorated and the food rations

were reduced. When Casement visited the camp
again in January 1915, he was not well received,
with men cat-calling, "How much are the
Germans paying you?"

Joseph wasn't remotely tempted
to join the Irish Brigade. As far as he
was concerned the Germans were
the enemy who had already killed
comrades of his, and he would rather
sit out the war in a POW camp than
betray the men he had fought alongside in the trenches. He hoped the
fighting would soon be over so that
he could get back home and carry
on with his life.

A Life in Service

By the start of the war, Mary Fearon was
twenty-nine years old and although she
had a suitor, she knew she was getting
rather old to marry. She had been born into
a farming family in Faughart, Dundalk, County
Louth, birthplace of Saint Brigid, the patron saint of
babies and fecundity, but Mary seemed destined to a life
without children. After leaving school, she worked in domestic
service, beginning as a scullery maid and working her way up to
the position of cook. She served in stately homes in County Louth
and County Down, and during the war was working for the Oswald
family at Haldane Grange in the wealthy seaside Dublin suburb of
Killiney. There she became friendly with a parlor maid, a girl
named Theresa.

ABOVE
*Mary Fearon (right) with
her sister Catherine. She
had worked in domestic
service at many stately
homes before coming to
Haldane Grange, Killiney.*

Mary's family members were ardent Republicans, strongly in
favor of home rule for Ireland. Just before the war, the Third Home
Rule Act had been on the verge of passing into law, but was
vehemently opposed by Unionists in the north, who formed a
militia called the Ulster Volunteers, while Nationalists in the south
formed the rival Irish Volunteers. John Redmond, leader of the
Nationalist Party, urged his supporters to fight in the war in order
to defend small countries such as Belgium. Some Nationalists did
volunteer but the proportion of men enlisting was much lower

RIGHT
A postcard from Joseph to Mary sent from Limburg. Prisoners were told to instruct their families that they should not write too often and letters should be short, clear, and legible so that the camp censors could make them out.

than in Scotland, England, and Wales, and the more radical Nationalists were strongly against fighting for the British army. In July 1915, the Catholic Church condemned the war, urging all sides to seek a peaceful solution, and voluntary recruitment in Ireland dropped further. Stories circulated of discrimination against Irish soldiers by British commanders, and the news leaked out that a much higher proportion of Irish soldiers than British soldiers had been court-martialed and shot. All of this fed straight into the hands of rebel Nationalists. Some entered into direct negotiations with the German high command, who sent them a ship full of weapons, the SMS *Limbau*, which was intercepted by the Royal Navy before reaching Ireland.

The tide of opinion was turning against those Irishmen fighting with the British army, but all the same when Theresa Heape asked her friends in Killiney to write to her brother Joseph, Mary Fearon took up her pen. Joseph was only allowed to write two letters a month and one postcard a week. The letters he received were censored, and if a food parcel was sent from Ireland, it had to weigh less than 10 pounds and even then, more often than not, it didn't get through. The men were on reduced rations once they had turned down Casement's offer, and their misery was further compounded by a tuberculosis epidemic in the camp which Joseph feared catching. Mary was a good-hearted woman who wrote cheerful, chatty letters to try and bolster his morale, and they soon became warm friends. These letters have not survived, but there's no doubt they brightened Joseph's days a little as one year of imprisonment stretched into the next. At the beginning of the war, everyone had believed it would be over by Christmas. The

Catholic priests at Limburg encouraged the men to trust in God, but for Joseph that became harder as the years passed.

Homecoming

Conditions at Limburg got worse as food shortages hit the entire German nation, and 3 percent of all men held in prisoner-of-war camps would die of starvation and disease before the Armistice on November 11, 1918. Joseph survived, though, and was formally discharged from the army on December 15, 1918; he was home in time for Christmas. He had lost most of his body weight and was suffering from bronchitis, but that still made him one of the lucky ones, as few of the other BEF soldiers who had traveled out to France in August 1914 had made it to the war's end. One of the first things Joseph did was travel to Killiney to see his sister Theresa and to meet Mary face to face.

EASTER UPRISING

On April 24, 1916 a group of about 1,800 Nationalists, led by James Connolly and Patrick Pearse, seized key buildings in Dublin, including the General Post Office, and proclaimed Ireland a republic. The British government dispatched 8,000 troops to crush the rebellion and, during the six-day battle that followed, the city suffered extensive damage and 466 people were killed, most of them civilians caught in crossfire. At first the rebels had little public support, but the execution of fifteen of their leaders transformed them into martyrs, as a result of which support grew for Irish independence. Radical Nationalists comprehensively defeated the more moderate Nationalists at the 1918 general election, sparking the War of Independence that eventually led to the establishment of the Irish Free State in 1922. Éamon de Valera, a leader of the Uprising, escaped execution on a technicality and went on to become a key party leader, head of government, and president of Ireland during his long political career.

LEFT
The Daily Sketch *of May 3, 1916, shows the General Post Office on Dublin's Sackville Street burning out of control.*

The mutual affection they had formed through their correspondence did not diminish on meeting, and they began to go out together on her afternoons off work. She often brought home-cooked food for him to build up his strength after the starvation he had endured in the camp. However, her family and friends took a dim view of the relationship. Far from being seen as war heroes, men who had fought for the British army were now, in the post-1916 climate, viewed as traitors. Tom Kettle, a former Nationalist MP who had been killed at the Battle of the Somme, had predicted that the leaders of the 1916 Uprising "will go down in history as heroes and martyrs; and I will go down—if I go down at all—as a bloody British officer." And he was right. Soldiers returning to Nationalist areas faced insults, threats, and actual violence. Joseph kept his head down and avoided speaking about his wartime experiences, because during the War of Irish Independence (1919–22) most ex-servicemen faced harassment.

Still, Mary was determined not to let the injustice of the accusations put her off. Joseph was Irish through and through and had chosen to fight for the British army to better his prospects. When he proposed marriage, she accepted, and the ceremony took place at

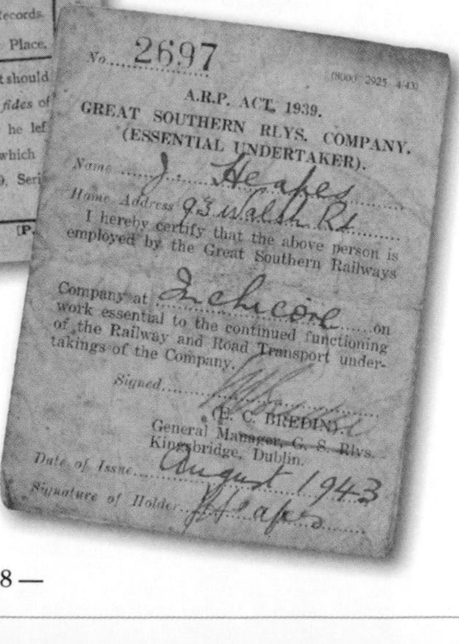

BELOW
Joseph's certificate of discharge from the army. He had served for ten years and nine months with "exemplary character."

Serial No. 26. Records, XI District Army Form B. 2067.
NOTE.—The character given on this Certificate is based on holder's conduct throughout his military career.

Character Certificate of No. 8265 Rank Lance Corporal

Name Heapes Joseph
Surname / Christian Names in full

Unit and Regiment or Corps from which discharged: ROYAL IRISH RIFLES

This is to certify that the ex-soldier named above has served with the Colours for Ten years Nine months, and his character during this period was Exemplary

Signature and Rank
Officer i/c Infantry Records.

Date of discharge 15th Dec 1918. Dublin Place.

To safeguard the holder of this Certificate from impersonation it should be noted that, in the event of any doubt arising as to the *bona fides* of the bearer, reference should be made to the description, when he left the Colours, of the soldier to whom this Certificate was given, which recorded on his Discharge Certificate (Army Form B. 2079, Seri[al] No. 2028/83), and should be in his possession.

(A11310) Wt.W3166/RP2467. 150,000 7/10 Sch. 41. D.D. & L.

WARNING.—If this Certificate is lost a duplicate cannot be issued. You should therefore on no account part with it or forward it by post when applying for a situation, but should use a copy attested by a responsible person for the purpose.

to be issued without any alteration in the manuscript.

Police Issue Local Office No.

No. 2697

(8000) 2925 4/43

A.R.P. ACT. 1939.
GREAT SOUTHERN RLYS. COMPANY.
(ESSENTIAL UNDERTAKER).

Name J. Heapes
Home Address 93 Walsh Rd

I hereby certify that the above person is employed by the Great Southern Railways Company at Inchicore on work essential to the continued functioning of the Railway and Road Transport undertakings of the Company.

Signed
E. C. BREDIN.
General Manager, G. S. Rlys.
Kingsbridge, Dublin.

Date of Issue August 1943
Signature of Holder J Heapes

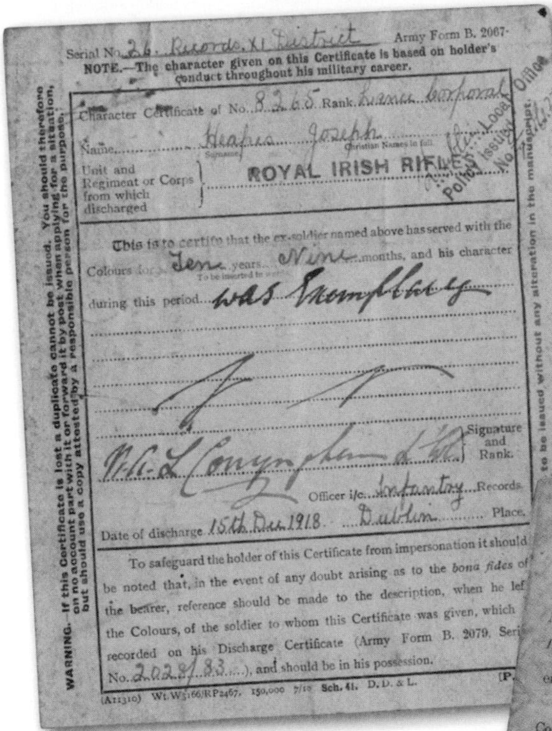

RIGHT
A card certifying Joseph's employment on the Great Southern Railways in 1943.

morning Mass on August 5, 1919, in the beautiful sandstone church of St. Alphonsus in Killiney, with Mary's sister Catherine as her bridesmaid. A reception was held afterward at the home of Mary's employers, Haldane Grange. Many friends would never speak to her again for marrying a man who fought for "the Brits," but she paid no heed to that; she was marrying the man she loved. In March 1921 her happiness was complete when she gave birth to a daughter, whom they named Elizabeth.

As the years went by, there was little recognition in Ireland of the Irishmen who had died in the war, and anyone attempting to sell poppies on Remembrance Day took their life in their hands. The Irish Civil War of 1922–23 concluded with Ireland being partitioned and most of it becoming the Irish Free State. Mary and Joseph moved to Dublin, where he obtained work with the Great Southern Railways in the gas-producing works at Inchicore.

Joseph died in 1972, twenty-six years before Queen Elizabeth II of England and President Mary McAleese of Ireland jointly unveiled a memorial at Messines in Belgium, honoring the spirit of all the Irishmen who fought in the First World War. As President McAleese said that day, "They fell victim to a war against oppression in Europe. Their memory too fell victim to a war for independence at home in Ireland." Joseph was one of the lucky ones; he got home and found the woman he wanted to spend the rest of his life with. Mary was lucky, too. Many Irishwomen of her generation never found husbands because, of the 210,000 Irishmen who went off to fight in the war, a sixth of them were dead before Armistice Day.

Joseph was one of the lucky ones: he got home and found the woman he wanted to spend the rest of his life with.

TOP
Mary and Joseph in the 1950s: After surviving the difficult years, they had a comfortable, happy life together.

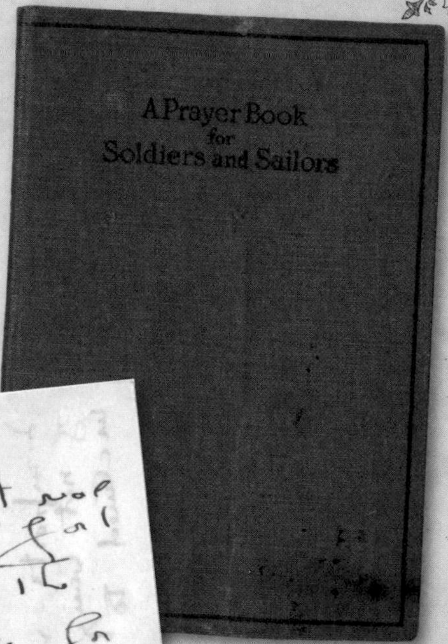

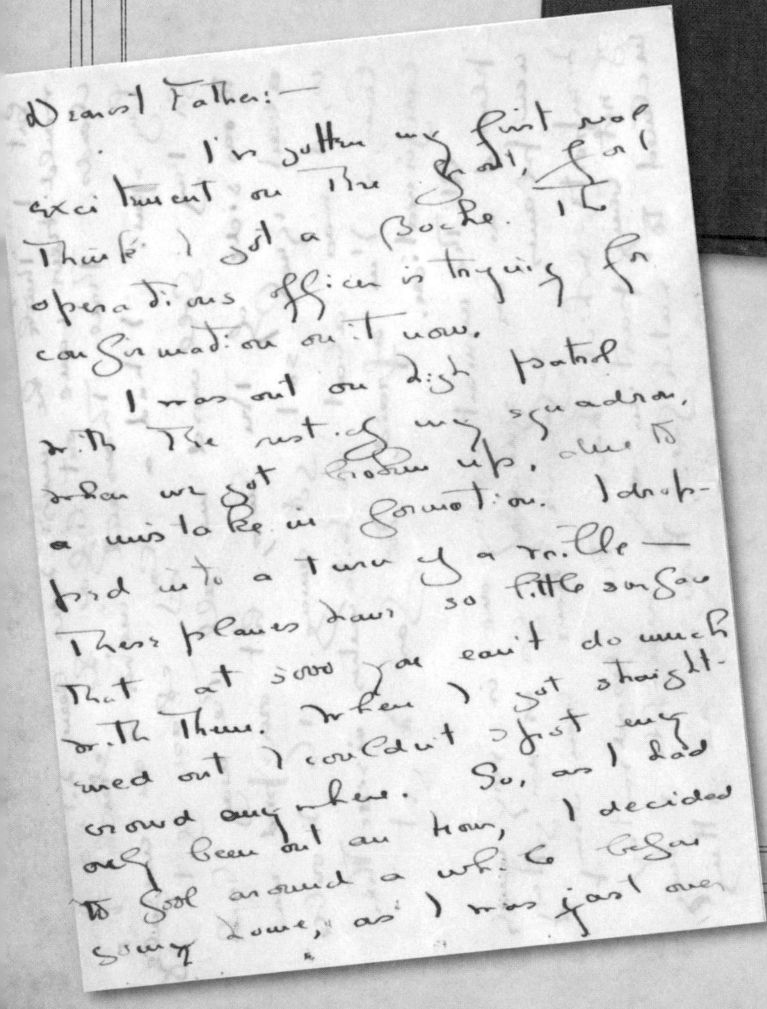

Quentin
ROOSEVELT
&
Flora
PAYNE WHITNEY

Quentin Roosevelt
AMERICAN

—

Born: November 19, 1897

—

Second lieutenant,
95th Aero Squadron

Flora Payne Whitney
AMERICAN

—

Born: July 27, 1897

ABOVE
*The young Quentin at the family home
in Sagamore Hill: He was brought up to
be a daredevil with a love of adventure
and the great outdoors.*

QUENTIN WAS AN EX-PRESIDENT'S SON AND FLORA A MILLIONAIRE'S DAUGHTER BUT NEITHER WAS REMOTELY SELF-IMPORTANT, AND THEIR LOVE FOR EACH OTHER, ACCORDING TO HER FRIEND IRENE, WAS "OF THE TRUEST AND MOST WONDERFUL KIND."

Quentin was the youngest of Theodore Roosevelt's six children and only three years old when his father became the 26th American President, a post he would hold throughout most of the first decade of the 20th century. Quentin was, according to his mother, a "fine bad little boy" who was always getting into mischief around the White House; his exploits included carving a baseball diamond into the White House lawn without permission, and throwing snowballs from the roof at Secret Service officers. He was quick-witted and imaginative and at Groton School in Massachusetts he edited the literary magazine and penned some rather macabre short stories. The Roosevelt brothers (Ted, Kermit, and Archie) were fiercely competitive and often challenged their younger sibling to feats of daring. One such challenge almost ended in disaster when Quentin jumped off a high rock into a deep-water cove near Oyster Bay, the hamlet on the North Shore of Long Island where the family's 23-room home, Sagamore Hill, was located. That was par for the course: from an early age all four brothers were raised to be courageous and to stand up for what they believed in.

BELOW
A family picnic at Oyster Bay, New York: Archie is on the left, Quentin and former president Theodore Roosevelt are in the foreground, and Edith, Quentin's mother, is to the right.

(FLORA PANE WHITNEY) 4636-1
MRS. RODERICK TOWER

ABOVE
*Flora had been
introduced to the king
and queen of England
through her father's
contacts in the world
of British horse-racing,
while her mother
introduced her to many
of the era's top artists.*

Flora was the eldest child of Harry Payne Whitney, heir to a family fortune earned in business and thoroughbred horseracing. Her mother, Gertrude Vanderbilt Whitney, was heir to an even greater fortune, and an aspiring sculptor as well as being a patron to other artists. Young Flora was brought up by governesses at the family homes in New York's Fifth Avenue and at the 700-acre Long Island estate of Westbury, as well as houses in Newport (Rhode Island), the Adirondacks, South Carolina, and Saratoga (New York State). It was a life of fabulous wealth, involving wild parties, gambling, and sporting fixtures, especially horse racing. Flora attended Brearley School in New York, and then Foxcroft School for Girls in Virginia, where she formed friendships she would keep for life. She made her debut into society at the family's Westbury home on August 4, 1916 and immediately started stepping out with Quentin, a neighbor on Long Island whom she had known since childhood. The young Roosevelt was studying mechanical engineering at Harvard, but he and Flora would see each other during the holidays and kept in touch during term time. He sent her dozens of postcards with newspaper cartoons stuck on them, as well as witty telegrams:

"Flora: am in imminent danger of relapsing into barbarism," he wrote, after accidentally leaving his shaving things behind at Westbury. On one occasion he drank too much and "acted as no gentleman should," so he telegrammed a profuse apology and promised he would abstain from drink for as long as she chose. Three months later he was still on the wagon and regretting his promise!

Quentin was somewhat wary of taking Flora home to meet his parents, who were disapproving of the ostentatious lifestyle of the Whitneys and didn't consider them to be people of substance. However,

She made her debut into society ... and immediately started stepping out with Quentin ...

when they did meet her in spring 1917 they liked her straightaway. She was thoughtful and quiet, and his father approved of the fact that her younger brother Sonny was training as an aviator while her cousin Caspar was training with the infantry. He had long campaigned against President Wilson's strategy of neutrality in the war, saying that "Unless men are willing to fight and die for great ideals, including love of country, ideals will vanish and the world will become one huge sty of materialism." When America eventually entered the war, he campaigned vigorously for increased funding for equipment and weapons, and donated large sums himself. His own sons Theodore, Archie, and Kermit had already signed up and in early summer of 1917 young Quentin enrolled at Mineola flying school. He had poor eyesight but overcame this handicap by memorizing the eye chart so that he would pass his physical exam. Around this time he asked Flora to marry him, and she joyously accepted his proposal.

All too soon, on July 23, 1917, Quentin was dispatched to continue his flying training in France. His mother accompanied him to his ship at the 14th Street Wharf in Manhattan, and Flora

THE "LUSITANIA"

On April 22, 1915 the German government issued a warning to civilians not to travel on the *Lusitania*, a passenger ship traveling from New York to Liverpool, but still 1,265 passengers and 694 crew set sail on May 1. The ship was the world's fastest trans-atlantic steamer, which everyone thought could dodge the Kaiser's U-boats. Besides, surely the Germans wouldn't strike at a civilian ship, would they? But on May 7, 11.5 miles off the coast of Ireland, the *Lusitania* was hit by a single torpedo fired from submarine *U-20* and sank a mere 18 minutes later. There was only time to launch six lifeboats and by the time rescue ships arrived, 1,195 people had perished, among them Flora's uncle, Alfred Gwynne Vanderbilt, who was on his way to Britain to inspect some racehorses. In the outcry that followed, the public began to realize that Theodore Roosevelt had been right to warn that neutrality wouldn't work. On May 8, the *New York Herald* headline read, "What a Pity Theodore Roosevelt is not President."

LEFT
Early news reports of the sinking of the Lusitania *underestimated the number of casualties.*

ABOVE
Archie and Quentin Roosevelt at military training camp while at Harvard, 1915/16. The uniforms they wore and the archaic rifles they fired were left over from the Spanish–American war, but it was thought important that students prepared for war.

sailed in on the Whitney yacht to say goodbye. She sprinkled a little bottle of salt water on his uniform, a tradition supposed to bring luck, and was "wonderfully brave" as she sat waiting with him for the ship to sail. He wrote to Flora from mid-Atlantic, saying, "If I am not killed, there will be a time when I shall draw into New York again, and you will be there on the pier, just as you were when I left, and there will be no parting for us for a long time to come."

Flying over France

When Quentin arrived in Issoudun, near Bourges, on August 14, 1917 he was appointed supply officer for the American flying school there. Eddie Rickenbacker, America's most successful flying ace, was the engineering officer and hugely admired by all the men. In the States Quentin had trained on an antiquated plane known as the Curtiss Jenny, but he now had to learn to fly a more modern French pursuit plane, the Nieuport 28. But even these were not the most up-to-date technology, as the French used a sturdier Spad S.XIII and the Nieuports were their cast-offs. Quentin had to learn evasive acrobatics, and he wrote to his mother that "The French monitors make us do all the wild flying stunts that were considered tom fool tricks back home." He also had to learn to fly in formation, which was no mean feat in "a hundred and twenty horsepower kite." He attended the aerial gunning school at Cazaux to learn how to fire a machine gun while flying, then went back to Issoudun as quartermaster, a role in which he excelled.

It was a wet autumn followed by a freezing winter and Quentin succumbed to pneumonia. Luckily, an old school friend of Flora's, Irene Givenwilson, was working nearby in France as a Red Cross nurse and was able to take care of him in his own bunk rather than send him off to the local hospital where he might have been exposed to other infections. When he was well enough, he traveled up to Paris to stay with his sister-in-law Eleanor in the house of an aunt of hers near the Bois de Boulogne; it was here that he spent Christmas recuperating from the illness.

Meanwhile, Flora had become a frequent visitor at Sagamore Hill, where she let Quentin's mother, Ethel, read any letters from her son that were not too romantic; in the process the two women became close friends. When Theodore Roosevelt went to Canada to promote war bonds, Flora accompanied him. She wrote to Quentin that she was terrified while his father stood on a stage making his speech because it made him an easy target for any assassin. Afterwards, Ethel wrote to Quentin that "the family were all perfectly devoted to her and thought her a very fine person." To Flora, Ethel wrote, "His love for you has made a man of Quentin. Before it came to him he was just a dear boy."

In March 1918, Quentin's brothers were making names for themselves: Archie, seriously injured in action, was awarded the highest French military honor, the Croix de Guerre; Kermit was awarded the British Military Cross for "exemplary gallantry" in an offensive against the Turks at Tikrit in Iraq; and Ted was in command of the 26th Regiment of the American First Division. The competitive spirit in which the Roosevelt brothers had been raised came to the fore, and Ted let Quentin know they considered him "a slacker" because he hadn't yet seen any action. It was very unfair. The reason Quentin hadn't seen front-line action was the shortage of planes, but Quentin was still ashamed and wrote to Flora saying, with customary modesty, "I am a very, very ordinary person I am afraid." She was "boiling with rage" when she got his letter and related its contents to Ethel, who was furious with Ted. In an act of moral support, Theodore also cabled Quentin: "If you have erred

BELOW
A photographer takes shots of a Nieuport 28: The French no longer used them because of their fragility, but they were at least easy to maneuver.

FLYING ACES

French newspapers first used the term "ace" in 1915 about pilot Adolphe Pégoud after he downed his fifth German plane; five came to be the generally accepted number you needed to shoot down to be considered a "flying ace." It was not always easy to confirm hits, but it was universally accepted that German pilot Manfred von Richthofen, otherwise known as the Red Baron, was responsible for shooting down 80 planes before he was himself brought down near the Somme in April 1918. René Fonck was the most famous French air ace with 75 "kills," and he also managed to survive the war. Billy Bishop of Canada brought down 72 planes, and Edward Mannock was the UK's highest scorer with 61, while Eddie Rickenbacker was America's most successful with 26.

ABOVE
Manfred von Richthofen, the infamous Red Baron.

at all it is in trying too hard to get to the front . . . We are exceedingly proud of you."

All the same, Quentin began to put pressure on his superior officers to let him fly in combat. Knowing his life would be on the line, he asked if it were possible for Flora to come over to France and marry him. She could live in the Paris house with his sister-in-law Eleanor, and he'd be able to see her during his time off duty. Flora began to explore this possibility only to discover a law prohibiting the sisters of servicemen from leaving the country during wartime. Theodore was furious. He thought she should have been allowed to go, "then, even if [Quentin] were killed, she and he would have known their white hours," he wrote. He put pressure on the War Department over that summer but to no avail.

Irene Givenwilson was still stationed at Issoudun, and Quentin liked being able to talk to her about Flora. When he got letters from his fiancée, Irene recalled, he would burst in "like an avalanche . . . and dance round the room waving them aloft." Irene told Flora she was "enshrined in Quentin's heart," his "guiding star." One evening they had a serious conversation in which Quentin told Irene about his wishes in the event that he were "bumped off:" "Fouf [Flora] has so much spunk, and she knows just how I would want her to act," he told her. "She must live on. Life is glorious."

Airborne at Last

In mid-June 1917, Quentin at last got his orders for combat flying. He was extremely popular in Issoudun and all the mechanics lined up to say goodbye, adding, "Let us know if you are captured and we will come and get you." There had never been any airs and graces about him. Rickenbacker described him as "Gay, hearty and absolutely square in everything he said or did . . . one of the most popular fellows in the group." Privately, some had concerns that he might be too much of a daredevil and wouldn't take sufficient care of himself in the air, but any such thoughts weren't voiced at the time.

Quentin was sent to the airfield at Orly, near Paris, where he joined the 95th Aero Squadron. After his first flight, he wrote to Flora "It is really exciting at first when you see the stuff bursting in great black puffs around you." And to his mother he wrote, "You get so excited that you forget about everything except getting the other fellow and trying to dodge the traces." On July 11, he downed his first German plane after a dogfight in which he evaded two others. But on the 14th his luck changed when a group of Nieuports in which he was flying encountered a larger group of Fokkers, commanded by Hermann Göring. Quentin was at the back in what was known as "tail-end Charlie" position, and he broke off from the formation in order to confront the pursuers. After a brave duel with a Fokker he took two machine-gun bullets in the back of the head and his plane hurtled to the ground near Chaméry, west of Reims.

Rumors of his death circulated straightaway, but it was July 20 before official news was received at Sagamore Hill, where Flora was staying with the Roosevelts. "Little Flora is broken-hearted," Theodore wrote to Archie. "I bitterly regret that he was not married and does not leave his own children behind him." Letters of condolence flooded in, including messages from King George V and from Allied leaders including Clemenceau, Balfour, and Lloyd George.

BELOW
Photographs of Quentin's body lying alongside the wreck of his plane were sent to the Roosevelts. So proud were they of their brave son that they had prints made to give to relatives.

> "*Flora dear, you will never realize how deeply he loved you.*"

Flora also received hundreds of letters, including one from Irene Givenwilson that read, "He used to dream of going home next year & marrying you . . . Flora dear, you will never realize how deeply he loved you." The last letters Quentin sent before his death arrived, among them a cheerful birthday greeting for the family's maid, Mary Sweeney.

The Germans realized who Quentin was and buried him with full military honors. Moreover, controversy was soon stirred up because the son of an ex-American president had been killed in battle yet the German Kaiser kept his six sons protected behind the lines. It was one more reason why German soldiers became disillusioned with the war that summer, and by the end of August 1918 they were beginning to desert in their thousands. After a German retreat that autumn, Quentin's grave was on the Allied side of the front line, and so many soldiers came to pay their respects that a protective barrier had to be erected around it.

ABOVE
Soldiers paying their respects at Quentin's grave in a field near Chamery.

Life Goes On . . . Eventually

Flora was inconsolable in her loss, but selflessly spent time with the Roosevelts, trying as best she could to comfort Quentin's mother. She was there when someone sent a photograph of Quentin's body alongside his mangled plane, but far from being upset by it Theodore pinned it on his wall to show how proud he was of his son. Later, they also displayed the crumpled axle of his plane recovered from the crash site.

For a long time, Flora did not socialize at all, but in 1920 she entered into a hasty marriage with one of Quentin's old comrades from Issoudun, a man called Roderick Tower. "Poor child," Ethel wrote. "I think she has just done it in desperation; she was so unhappy." It does seem as though Flora was looking for a replacement for Quentin, and although the couple had two children together, the marriage failed and the divorce in 1925 cited both Tower's drinking and his infidelities. Two years later Flora was married again, this time happily, to an architect called George Macculloch "Cully" Miller. Then in 1941 she became president of the Whitney Museum of American Art, which her mother had founded ten years earlier.

As Quentin had wished, she lived her life to the full, but there must have been days when she looked back on her first love, the witty, tender-hearted man who stole her heart at the age of nineteen. No doubt she daydreamed about what might have been if she had been able to enjoy her "white hours" with the president's son.

LEFT
Flora, c.1919. It took her many years to get over the loss of her dashing fiancé.

J R.R. & Edith
TOLKIEN

Married: March 22, 1916

**John Ronald Reuel
Tolkien**

BRITISH

—

Born: January 3, 1892

—

*Rank & regiment:
Lieutenant, Lancashire Fusiliers
then BEF 11th Battalion*

Edith Mary Bratt

BRITISH

—

Born: January 21, 1889

ABOVE
Edith and J.R.R. in 1961: Their relationship had
survived many separations and vicissitudes, but
they always had great affection for each other.

ACCORDING TO TOLKIEN, HE AND EDITH RESCUED EACH OTHER
FROM "THE DREADFUL SUFFERINGS OF OUR CHILDHOODS," AND THAT
CREATED A BOND SO STRONG THAT IT WOULD SEE THEM THROUGH
THE SEPARATIONS AND "DARKNESSES" OF THEIR LIVES.

E dith Bratt was illegitimate. Her father's name was known
to the Bratt family, but was not recorded on Edith's birth
certificate and they never revealed the secret to outsiders.
She grew up in Handsworth, Birmingham, with her mother, Frances,
and a cousin, Jennie Grove. From an early age she proved to be
a talented piano player. The family hoped she might one day
become a concert pianist, but her world fell apart after her mother
died suddenly when Edith was just nine years old. Her guardian,
the family solicitor, sent the grieving young girl to boarding school,
where she was desperately lonely. After she left school, he found a
room for her in a boarding house where the landlady, Mrs. Faulkner,
encouraged her to play the piano to entertain other guests, but
complained if she tried to practice during the day. It seemed as if
her dreams of being a professional musician were destined to
come to nothing.

BELOW
*A map of Birmingham
at the beginning of the
century. More than half
its men (150,000) served
in the war; 13,000 of
them were killed and
35,000 wounded.*

> *... during the summer of 1909 both admitted they had fallen in love.*

Edith was nineteen years old when two new lodgers arrived in the house—Ronald and Hilary Tolkien, sixteen and fourteen respectively. They had been born in South Africa, but moved back with their mother, Mabel, to live in England after their father died in 1895. Mabel encouraged her boys in a love of literature and language, and she also brought them up in the Roman Catholic faith after she herself converted in 1900, an act which caused her Baptist family to disown her. When Mabel died in 1905, Father Francis Morgan of the Birmingham Oratory was named as the boys' guardian and he was the one who oversaw their schooling and care. At first they lived with a childless aunt, Beatrice, but were unhappy there, so in 1908 Father Francis arranged for them to move into the lodging house where Edith lived.

Edith and Ronald took to each other straightaway, despite the fact that she was three years older. They formed an alliance against the strict landlady, whom they called "The Old Lady," and persuaded the maid to smuggle them extra food from the kitchen. They sat in Birmingham tea shops giggling as they threw sugar lumps at passers-by and, during the summer of 1909, both admitted they had fallen in love. Tolkien wrote to her in later life recalling "your first kiss to me (which was almost accidental)—and our goodnights when sometimes you were in your little white night-gown, and our absurd long window talks." He was supposed to be studying for his Oxford entrance exam that summer, but took time off to spend with Edith instead. After they went on a day-long bicycle ride in the autumn of 1909, word of the budding romance reached Father Francis, who reacted with fury, banning them from seeing each other and moving Ronald and Hilary to new lodgings.

Upset by the enforced breakup, Edith accepted an invitation to go and

BELOW
The Barrow's cafe in Birmingham: Tolkien and his friends used to meet here as a group calling themselves The Tea Club or The Barrovian Society, which they later reduced to the acronym T.C.B.S. Only two of them would survive the war.

live with friends in Cheltenham, and Father Francis forbade Ronald from even so much as writing to her, saying that he could do as he wished when he turned twenty-one, but that until then he must do as he was told. That was still three years hence, a desperately long separation for an ardent young lover, but he felt he had no choice but to obey.

True Love Wins the Day

As Tolkien later wrote about the ban, "Probably nothing else would have hardened the will enough to give such an affair (however genuine a case of true love) permanence." He obeyed Father Francis, going to Oxford to study Classics and then switching to English Language and Literature, but on January 2, 1913, on the eve of his twenty-first birthday, he wrote to Edith telling her he still loved her and asking when they might be reunited. A devastating reply came by return. She said that she'd believed Ronald had forgotten all about her and had therefore become engaged to a man called George Field. Edith had made a new life for herself in Cheltenham, playing piano at the Baptist Church and forming a number of close friendships, among them one with this man George, the brother of a school friend.

ABOVE
Ronald, aged nineteen, while a student at Oxford during his enforced three-year separation from Edith.

Tolkien would not take "no" for an answer. On January 8, he caught a train to Cheltenham where he and Edith spent the day walking in the countryside and talking about their situation. He must have been persuasive because by the end of the day she had agreed to break off her engagement to George Field and marry Ronald instead.

They decided not to announce their engagement right away. Tolkien wanted to complete his education and establish a way to earn enough of a living to support Edith. One other matter stood in the way, and that was religion. He asked her to convert to Catholicism so they could be married in the Catholic Church and,

CONSCRIPTION IN WORLD WAR ONE

Most German states had introduced compulsory military service back in the early 19th century, so when war began in 1914 they had a well-trained army of 3.5 million regulars, conscripts, and reservists. France had only 1.1 million, but they raised more after 1912 by extending the length of military service to three years and drafting 84 percent of all eligible men. The draft was not introduced in Britain during the first half of the war because public opinion was set against it. During the six months after war was declared, a million men volunteered to fight, but many more were required as the casualty rate was so much higher than expected. The famous British Lord Kitchener posters reading, "Your Country Needs You" were widely distributed and popular songs encouraged enlistment. Still the number of volunteers was not sufficient and in January 1916 the British government was forced to introduce conscription, targeting single men first and then married ones. In America only 73,000 volunteered in the first six weeks after they entered the war, so in June 1917 Woodrow Wilson introduced the draft for those aged 21 to 31 (a range later broadened to 18 to 45).

RIGHT
Lord Kitchener, Secretary of State for War, was a commanding presence on British recruitment posters.

reluctantly, she agreed. On January 8, 1914, she was accepted into the Catholic Church but at a price: the friends with whom she had been living asked her to leave their house, and she also had to give up her piano playing at the Baptist Church and attend the rather more dour Catholic ceremonies instead. She and Ronald quarreled about it, though they never fell out for long. He had begun writing stories and poems, including some written especially for her: "we have become/as one, deep-rooted in the soil/of Life, and tangled in sweet growth."

Tolkien decided not to volunteer when the war began, opting to finish his degree instead, but after graduating in June 1915

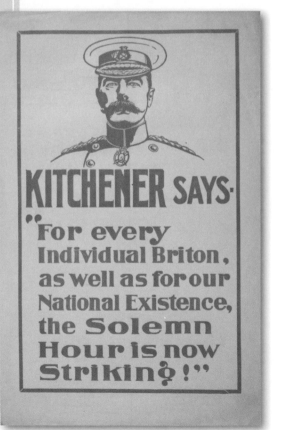

KITCHENER SAYS-
"For every Individual Briton, as well as for our National Existence, the Solemn Hour is now Striking!"

with first class honors, he took up a commission in the Lancashire Fusiliers and began his training. Edith was now living in Warwick with her cousin Jennie, and Ronald bought a motorcycle so he could ride down to visit her during his periods of leave. He became the battalion's signaling officer and had to learn Morse code, flag signaling, how to handle carrier pigeons, and how to use a field telephone. They knew it wouldn't be long before he was sent to France, so on March 22, 1916, he and Edith were married at the Catholic Church in Warwick. When it was time to sign the register, she had a problem as it asked for the name, rank, and profession of her father, and she had never told Ronald of her illegitimacy. Flustered, she scribbled down the name of an uncle, but later when she told Ronald the truth, he replied, "I think I love you even more tenderly because of all that."

They honeymooned for a week in Somerset, but this was marred somewhat by press speculation about an imminent "Big Push" by the British army. Both knew that Ronald would be a part of it.

Trench Fever

Tolkien arrived in France on June 6, 1916, and found on arrival that all his gear had been stolen, which seemed an inauspicious start. He was transferred to the 11th Battalion and hung around for three weeks until they set off for the Somme, marching through torrential downpours past villages where the buildings were mere piles of

BELOW
Soldiers going "over the top" on July 1, 1916, during the Battle of the Somme. A bell rang to signal when it was time to climb out of the trenches and into the line of enemy fire.

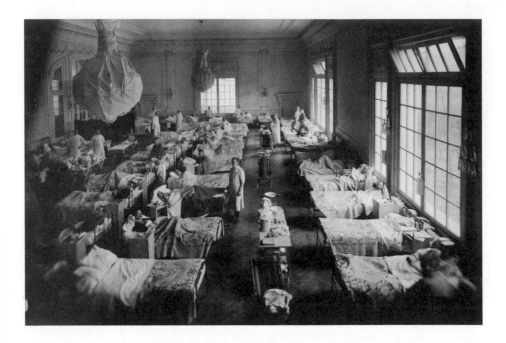

rubble. On July 1, the first British troops went "over the top" in what became known as the Battle of the Somme, but Tolkien's battalion was held in reserve. This was lucky for him, because 20,000 Allied troops were killed that first day alone. It wasn't until July 14 that his unit was sent forward to the Front. First they tried unsuccessfully to capture the little village of Ovillers from the Germans, with Tolkien frustrated at the poor state of the communications systems, few of which were functioning efficiently. Next they stormed the German stronghold of Schwaben Redoubt where several prisoners were taken. Many of his unit were killed, but he survived unscathed.

Back home Edith was frantic with worry. She received regular letters from him, written in a prearranged code they knew she could decipher so as to work out where he was along the Western Front. But then she read the news reports and realized that he was in one of the most dangerous spots in the entire theater of war. Between July 1 and November 18, more than a million men would die at the Somme, making it one of the bloodiest battles ever fought. Every knock on the door might mean a telegram announcing her husband's death.

Instead, on October 27, 1916, Tolkien succumbed to trench fever, a serious disease that caused extreme, flu-like symptoms. He was admitted to a field hospital in France, but his condition did not improve, so in November he was shipped back to a hospital in Birmingham, where Edith arrived for a joyful reunion. Although thin and still very weak, he was discharged from hospital in time to spend Christmas with her. During his convalescent leave he began writing a story called "The Fall of Gondolin," which Edith copied out for him. Before he could finish it, however, in April 1917 he was passed fit to return to the Front, then fell ill again before he could be shipped out and was forced to return to the hospital. For the remainder of the war, he alternated between spells in the hospital and spells on garrison duty, but was never deemed healthy enough to go back to France. He was extremely fortunate because the 11th Battalion had been almost completely wiped out by the war's end. Chances are he would not have survived.

In November 1917, after a difficult and at times life-threatening labor, Edith gave birth to their first child, a son they called John. Tolkien couldn't get leave to be there for the birth, but he came to the

DISEASE IN THE TRENCHES

Trenches were overrun by rats and all kinds of insect life, so disease and infection were rife. The men were prone to cholera from contaminated food or water and dysentery from bacteria or parasites. Many chose to shave their heads to avoid the incessant, infuriating itching caused by nits. Trench foot, a fungal infection caused by prolonged standing around in cold, wet conditions, made the feet swell up and lose sensation. In severe cases it could cause gangrene, and amputation of the toes was sometimes necessary. Doctors were initially puzzled by the disease they called "trench fever," whose symptoms included headaches, high fever, skin rashes, inflamed eyes, and acute pains in the legs. Most cases cleared up after a few weeks of bed rest, but some (like Tolkien's) were more severe and kept recurring. It was only in 1918 that medics realized the disease was being spread by the bites of lice, which laid their eggs in the seams of clothing and were extremely hard to eradicate.

christening some weeks later, conducted by Father Francis, his old guardian. One day Tolkien and Edith went walking in some woods and Edith did a little dance for him in a clearing. He later recalled: "Her hair was raven, her skin clear, her eyes bright, and she could sing—and dance." This episode became the inspiration for a character called Lúthien, an immortal elf-maid who would be at the center of his novel *The Silmarillion*, and Arwen, a half-elven creature in *The Lord of the Rings*. Years later he wrote to his son explaining the deep personal significance of that day: "For ever (especially when alone) we still met in the woodland glade and went hand in hand many times to escape the shadow of imminent death before our last parting."

Although Tolkien had spent only four months in France, it was long enough to feel the shadow of the war's "oppression," and he later wrote that he was glad to have seen that place where men of all backgrounds and types were thrown together. But by 1918, all but one of his closest friends from university had been killed.

ABOVE
Tolkien in the 1940s, while he was an Oxford University professor. He was trained to work as a code breaker during the Second World War, but was never called upon.

BELOW
According to Tolkien, the Dead Marshes he describes in Lord of the Rings *"owe something to Northern France after the Battle of the Somme."*

After the War

Tolkien and Edith's marital life did not begin properly until after the war, when he got a job as a lexicographer on the *New English Dictionary* in Oxford and they set up home. Edith wasn't particularly happy with the social life there, which she found very formal and intimidating. She was happier in 1920 when Tolkien took up a post at the University of Leeds, but by 1925 they were back in Oxford again by which time Tolkien had become preoccupied with his writing. Edith busied herself with playing the piano and caring for their children, of whom there would be four altogether— three boys and a girl. They argued over his preference for the company of his male friends, and over Catholicism, which she increasingly resented. The two began to lead quite separate lives, sleeping in separate rooms, but always remaining solicitous of the other's comfort.

Tolkien wrote long into the night and the results would make him one of the giants of English literature. *The Hobbit,* published in 1937, was an immediate success. *The Lord of the Rings* came out in three volumes in 1954 and 1955 and, despite its length and mixed reviews, became one of the most popular works of fiction of the 20th century. *The Silmarillion* was published posthumously in 1977.

After Tolkien retired from university work, he and Edith moved to Bournemouth, to a cottage she loved, and their old teenage closeness returned. They often sat in the evening on the veranda, where he smoked a pipe, she had a cigarette (having taken up smoking in old age), and they talked of their children and grandchildren. They had been through many difficult times—the wounds of childhood bereavement, the arguments and distance that sometimes affected their marriage—but, as Tolkien wrote in a letter to his son, Christopher, "these never touched our depths or dimmed the memories of our youthful love."

BELOW
Tolkien began work on The Silmarillion *while he was on sick leave during the war; two of his elven characters were inspired by Edith's singing and dancing.*

66 *... these difficult times never touched our depths or dimmed the memories of our youthful love.* 99

RIGHT
A letter from Lloyd dated February 16, 1919, when he was working for the postal service in Commercy, France.

BELOW
A standard-issue US first-aid kit. All US troops carried these tins containing two bandages to apply to the entry and exit wounds made by a bullet.

Lloyd & Mary
STALEY

Married: September 15, 1920

Lloyd Maywood Staley
AMERICAN

———

Born: September 10, 1895

———

Rank & regiment:
Private, Company K, 35th
Division US Army; then Sergeant
in US postal service

Mary Beatrice Gray
AMERICAN

———

Born: May 1, 1897

ABOVE
*Mary was both pretty and
clever, and many of the boys
at school were keen on her.*

LLOYD AND MARY HAD BEEN HIGH-SCHOOL SWEETHEARTS SINCE
1913, BUT HE DIDN'T ASK HER TO MARRY HIM BEFORE LEAVING FOR
FRANCE; HE THOUGHT HIS CHANCES OF RETURNING ALIVE WERE
"RATHER SLIM" AND DIDN'T WANT TO ENTER INTO A COMMITMENT
HE WOULD NOT BE ABLE TO HONOR.

M ary's father, George, was an itinerant preacher for the
Plymouth Brethren, an Evangelical movement whose
adherents believed in simple Christian observance
and worship, and had come from Scotland to the US in 1892 to
spread the word. Mary's mother's family came from Sweden and
had emigrated in the first half of the 19th century. The couple
were married in Kansas City in 1896, but moved around frequently
during Mary's childhood as her father sought new converts. They
lived in various parts of Nebraska, in Kansas City, and then in
Ottawa, Kansas, where Mary started junior high school in the fall
of 1911—and where she first met Lloyd.

Lloyd grew up on a farm south of Wellsville, Kansas, where the
year was punctuated by planting and harvesting, the care of livestock,
hunting rabbits and squirrels, and swimming on hot days in an old
swimming hole. He attended a small country school, and stayed
there an extra year beyond eighth grade because his older brother
Glen was still away at high school and only one boy could be

BELOW
*Lloyd's grandfather built
the farmhouse in Kansas
where Lloyd was born.*

spared from working on the farm at a time. When Lloyd's turn
came, he moved to Ottawa to live with his grandmother and
immediately thrived at Ottawa High School. He became captain
of the football team, president of his senior class, and was also
accepted into a literature society.

Mary was pretty and a lot of the boys were keen
on her when she joined the school, but by senior year
she and Lloyd had become an item. At the senior class
picnic, they loitered behind the rest of the crowd, and
Lloyd later told her that these were "golden days,"
the happiest of his entire school career. After leaving
school they continued to see each other whenever
they could, going to concerts and attending church
together as well as walking in the countryside, but her
family always returned to Nebraska for the summer,
so they got into the habit of writing to each other
during these periods of separation.

> *Mary must have
> been disappointed
> that he did not
> propose marriage to
> her before leaving.*

In 1916, Lloyd enrolled at Ottawa University and he was still a
freshman when on April 6, 1917, the United States formally entered
the First World War. In a burst of patriotism, he enrolled for the 1st
Company Kansas National Guard, a decision which, he wrote later,
after seeing the horrors of war first-hand, "I do not now believe was
done in the exercise of best judgment."

Mary must have been anxious at the news of his enlistment, and
disappointed that he did not propose marriage to her before leaving.
They had been courting for four years and she was already twenty
years old, which was quite an age to still be single in their generation.
There was no way of knowing how long he would be away from
home or if he would even return. On their last evening together,
August 4, 1917, they went out in his Ford motorcar and, according
to a letter he wrote from the Front, "the celebration was continued
into the early morning of the fifth." She saw him off at the station
and both agreed that they would write to each other regularly.
Thus began their long and very loving war correspondence.

Over to Europe

During the winter of 1917–18, Lloyd did his Army basic training at
Camp Doniphan, Oklahoma, in a tent heated only by a stove. It was
a cold snowy winter, with strong winds, and many a tent caught fire
when sparks from the stove struck the canvas. On April 24, 1918, the

WORLD WAR ONE SLANG

The use of slang terms at the front line encouraged a feeling of comradeship, and many phrases used then have made their way into the language. Germans were known as "Fritz," "Jerry," "Huns," or (by the French) "Boche;" they were said to find the last of these particularly rude. The French were "Parlewuhs" or "Parleyvoos" (from *parlez-vous*) or "Tulemongs" (*tout le monde*). British soldiers were universally known as "Tommies," a term said to be derived from a soldier who had distinguished himself at the Battle of Waterloo, while Americans were "doughboys," a word thought to have come from the Mexican–American war when forces were covered in chalky adobe dust. Lots of phrases denigrated superior officers, so the oak leaves on a field officer's hat became "scrambled eggs," while those with lightning decorations became "farts and darts," and any of high rank were known as "brass." "Blighty" was England (it derived from a Hindi word), so "a Blighty" was a wound serious enough to get you sent home. And no one directly referred to death but spoke of unlucky comrades "going west" or "hopping it."

ABOVE & LEFT
Propaganda posters were designed to aid recruitment and to raise funds to support the war effort. Buying liberty bonds, a type of investment that raised capital for the military, was seen as a patriotic duty in America.

regiment set sail from New York bound for Liverpool, with Lloyd writing of a rough crossing. But arriving in England, he found it to be "a very pretty country," though with "a noticeable lack of men." They caught a train down to the Channel coast, then sailed for France to begin further training under a British commander. Lloyd wrote to Mary that it was hard to believe they were so near the Front as they looked out over "peaceful-looking farming country," but then the big guns began, their sound echoing from one direction and then another.

BELOW
Lloyd on leave in southern France during 1919. He enjoyed sightseeing and collecting battlefield souvenirs, including a German Iron Cross medal.

Mary wrote that her brother Robert had volunteered for the Royal Flying Corps, the British Air Force. Lloyd commiserated with her on losing not one but two loved ones, but he told her he believed there would be two classes of men after the war, "the ones who went, and the ones who did not."

Wanting to be of some use, Mary volunteered for a Red Cross war drive in which she and other volunteers raised funds for the war effort. In the summer of 1918, she had to help getting in the harvest without the young men there to do it, and she wrote to Lloyd of the magnificent cherry harvest and that she was making his favorite cherry pies. In August she attended a "Chautauqua," a Methodist summer camp with lectures, music, and religious instruction, which she and Lloyd had attended together the year before. She wrote that she was considering going into nursing, and Lloyd replied that it was a fine career but hoped "that this fuss will all be over before you ever have to get into it."

He had also changed jobs, in June 1918 being transferred to work for the postal service. His letters started to become more and more affectionate, and perhaps this was because he was now in the Vosges mountains near the Front, close enough to see some casualties of war, and it was all beginning to seem much more real. In one letter, dated June 24, 1918, he says he wants to take Mary "in his arms and kiss those sweet rosy lips again," and that "someday we will be the happiest boy and girl that there possibly can be anywhere in the world." Was he proposing marriage to her? Surely that must be how Mary read it back home. He couldn't tell her where he was or the letter would be held back by the censors, but she followed the news of the war in the newspapers and must have been anxious for him

> " ... *someday we will be the happiest boy and girl that there possibly can be anywhere in the world.* "

BELOW
Looking across no-man's-land towards German lines in the Meuse-Argonne region. Lloyd's company suffered heavy losses when they advanced across this ground as part of the Grand Offensive of September 1918

THE GERMAN LINES, SHOWING HILL 304.

MAIL SERVICE OVERSEAS

Lloyd often complains in his letters that long stretches of time pass in which he receives no letters at all then four or five come at once after a mail ship docks. In fact, the addressing of army mail was a hit-and-miss business. Folks back home weren't allowed to know where their loved ones were in France, so they could only address letters or parcels to a soldier care of his company, and non-military folk were sometimes unaware of the need to be specific in the details; there were dozens of Company Ks or 4th Divisions. Soldiers' letters were supposed to be censored by the company commander so as to prevent sensitive information reaching enemy hands, while official censors did random checks on mail which could leave letters so mangled as to be illegible. British, French, and German troops generally got letters within a week of mailing, but for Americans, Canadians, Australians, and New Zealanders, it could be several weeks, so perishable goods sent in packages would arrive in unrecognizable condition. And in many cases, the family back home received letters from a soldier long after the telegram telling them of his death.

every time she read the rumors that American troops were going to be involved in a "Big Push."

Bit by bit, the 35th, Lloyd's company, were getting closer to the fighting, traveling across France almost to the Swiss border, and on September 26, 1918, they found themselves in the front line of an offensive at Meuse-Argonne. This was part of the Grand Offensive right up and down the Western Front, in which British, French, Canadian, Australian, and New Zealand troops who had survived thus far into the war were joined by the fresh wave of American troops and pushed forward against German lines. The strength and energy of this offensive is credited with demoralizing the Germans and bringing about the eventual surrender—though not without cost. Lloyd's company suffered more casualties than any other US division as they progressed through heavily defended regions, taking hundreds of German prisoners. Lloyd wasn't in battle with them because of his work for the postal service, but he wrote to Mary, "I have seen wounded men, my own soldiers in arms, coming back to the hospitals and, well, it just gets you." He drove around the country roads in transporter trucks and frequently saw "a blinding flash like a giant flash for photographic work" when a big shell landed in their vicinity, killing any who were close by. All around, the little towns they passed through had been reduced to rubble.

The Wait to get Home

In the fall of 1918, Mary's family moved back to Kansas City and she took a job as a reporter for the Kansas City News Service, which published a number of trade magazines. Lloyd wrote that he was sure it was more suited to her than nursing because the nurses he had seen in France were on the go all the time and had to be physically very strong. She loved the job and did well at it,

ABOVE
American soldiers
escorting German
prisoners in the Meuse-
Argonne. Conditions
for prisoners of war
were dictated by the
Hague and Geneva
Conventions agreed
upon before the war.

earning a pay increase. Lloyd wrote wistfully that he did not have a job to return to himself, having come into the war straight from school, but that after their work in France was done he would have more time to make plans. "It surely will be the happiest of happy days to be with you always," he wrote.

By October, Lloyd was lodging in Bourges in the house of a Frenchwoman who had a great big fireplace, a piano, and some antique chairs. In the evenings some African-American soldiers played piano and sang, and Lloyd wrote, "I don't believe I have enjoyed any music so much since coming across." When the Americans first joined the war, the English had told them that it would last at least another two years. No one predicted that it would be over by November 11 that year, so the news of the Armistice was greeted with great joy by the French. "They are certainly a happy lot of people," Lloyd wrote.

Lloyd would have liked to get home as soon as possible, but by December he had been told that he was going to be staying in France "until things are definitely settled." On Christmas Day 1918, he opened a box Mary had sent him and was delighted to find pictures of her and his mother, some talcum powder, toothpaste, and Hershey's candies, as well as gifts from the rest of the family. For Christmas dinner in the mess they had, "roast pork, mashed

In May 1919, Lloyd was sent back to the US and he wrote to Mary, "Home at last and now what is needed to make me the happiest man ever in Sam's army is to meet you and Mother."

potatoes, gravy, turnips, olives, pie, coffee, and bread"—a veritable feast.

On January 10, Lloyd wrote that they had spent seven days' leave in the town of Commercy, in the Meuse, and noted that there were "numerous pretty, well-dressed girls" there. He told Mary that some of the boys had "strayed" but that he had not because he knew he had a girl back home who was "true and faithful." He sent her gifts of French perfume and a pretty vase, which delighted her, and wrote that he had been collecting souvenirs of war, including a German Iron Cross.

The final weeks and months dragged by and it was April 1919 when Lloyd's unit finally sailed home and made their way to Camp Funston in Kansas. On May 2, he found out over breakfast that he was getting his discharge and was able to send a telegram to tell Mary, adding the news that he had just been promoted to sergeant.

A Long Engagement

Right after his discharge, Lloyd traveled to Kansas City to be reunited with his sweetheart, who had written to him faithfully and loyally right through the war. Having stuck by him, though, Mary was expecting a proposal of marriage on his return and when it was not forthcoming, she burst into tears one evening, then wrote him a very hurt letter. "I am just a big blundering idiot," he replied. He explained to her that he had not given her a ring before heading off to war in case he did not return, and promised that he would give her one the very next time he saw her. However, there was a condition: he couldn't actually marry her "until I can at least have a possibility of the home that you deserve."

Lloyd went back to work on his parents' farm that summer, then in September 1919 he enrolled at Gem City Business College in Quincy, Illinois. The school was forced to close during a coal strike, so he came back to work for Mary's father in a company that manufactured furniture for banks, then in a business that did some house building. Finally he married Mary on September 15, 1920, at her parents' home in Kansas City after what amounted to a seven-year courtship. As was the custom of the day, she gave up her job at the Kansas City News Service to be a homemaker, and he took over his parents' farm for a time before going to work for the US post office.

There were financial lean periods over the years, but Lloyd and Mary were blessed with eight children—five boys and three girls. Tragedy struck in February 1944 when their eldest son Warren was killed while piloting a B-25 bomber over Greece during the Second World War. The other children grew up and settled in California or Arizona, so Mary and Lloyd headed out to California after Lloyd's retirement to be near enough to spoil their grandchildren.

It took Lloyd a long time to get around to marrying the girl he had met back in high school, and he was very lucky that she waited for him. Mary was an attractive, strong-minded girl who could easily have found someone else. But in Lloyd's opinion, through all the corresponding they were forced to do in their courtship they "found a deeper love" than they might otherwise have enjoyed, and maybe that was the secret to their long and happy marriage.

BELOW
Lloyd and Mary, c. 1924, with two of their sons, John and Warren. Warren, their eldest boy, would be killed in February 1944 while serving as a pilot in the Second World War.

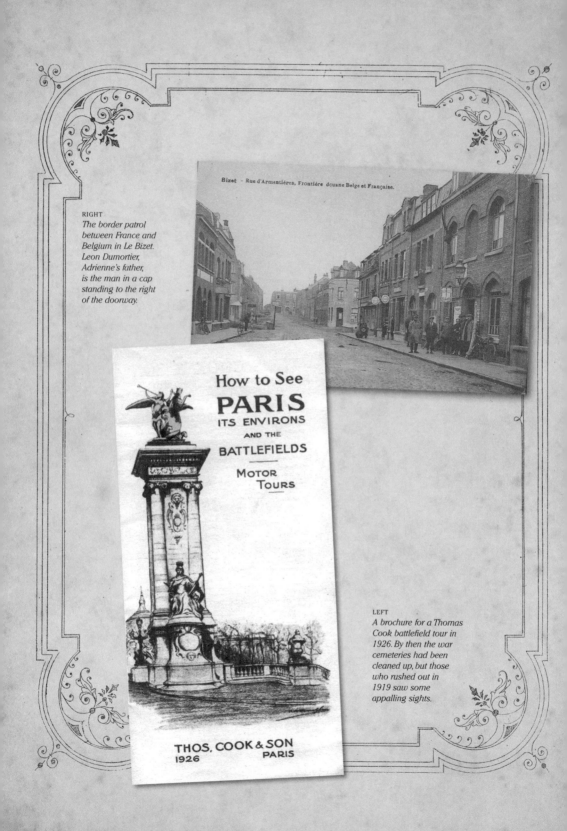

RIGHT
The border patrol between France and Belgium in Le Bizet. Leon Dumortier, Adrienne's father, is the man in a cap standing to the right of the doorway.

Bizet - Rue d'Armentiéres, Frontiére douane Belge et Française.

How to See
PARIS
ITS ENVIRONS
AND THE
BATTLEFIELDS

MOTOR
TOURS

THOS. COOK & SON
1926   PARIS

LEFT
A brochure for a Thomas Cook battlefield tour in 1926. By then the war cemeteries had been cleaned up, but those who rushed out in 1919 saw some appalling sights.

Jack & Adrienne
FOX

Married: November 24, 1919

John "Jack" Thomas Frederick Fox	Adrienne Marie Dumortier
BELGIAN	BELGIAN
—	—
May 7, 1891	*October 23, 1898*
—	—
Rank & regiment: *Private, Royal Artillery* *Regiment*	*War work:* *Munitions factory worker*

LEFT
Adrienne (seated front) and Rachel (standing behind her) with their sisters Yvonne, Alida, and Irma, and brothers Gaston and Maurice. This image was taken in Hazebrouck in 1919/20, after the family's return from the South of France.

BELOW
Jack with the Royal Artillery at Dover Barracks in 1915 after having been shipped back from Hong Kong. He is in the second row down, third from the left.

CLOSE TO THE WAR'S END, JACK FOX FELL IN LOVE WITH A PRETTY YOUNG FLEMISH GIRL CALLED RACHEL DUMORTIER. HE WANTED TO MARRY HER, BUT WHEN HER FAMILY FOUND OUT ABOUT THEIR AFFAIR THEY INSISTED HE MARRY HER ELDER SISTER ADRIENNE INSTEAD.

J ack was a shy, quiet lad who grew up in the village of Saxilby six miles west of Lincoln, England. His father died when he was ten and his mother got married again, to a local man who, like Jack's dad, worked as a farm laborer. There wasn't any other work to be had in the area so just before his eighteenth birthday, in 1909, Jack volunteered for the Royal Artillery in order to learn some skills and earn a living. He did his basic training at Dover Castle, where he learned from the start about the rigors of military life after he was reprimanded because his cap wasn't straight. In 1912 he was sent out to Hong Kong as part of a garrison defending the British colonial territory. He enjoyed the exotic culture there, buying himself some enameled vases with Chinese engravings and an imitation dagger. In 1914 and early 1915, the men listened with alarm to news reports as war was declared in Europe and the British Expeditionary Force suffered early setbacks. They knew they would inevitably become part of the fighting and, sure enough, in June 1915 they were shipped back, arriving in Northern France in December 1915.

BELOW
A dutiful son, Jack had this picture taken at a photographer's studio in France to send back to his mother in Lincoln.

Jack was first attached to the 41st Siege Battery, composed half of regulars from Hong Kong and Singapore and half of territorials from Durham. His job was loading and firing howitzers, a heavy kind of supergun that fired high-explosive shells, based on the northern edge of the Western Front, around Ypres, Arras, and the Somme. By 1917 he had been moved to the 63rd Siege Battery and was firing huge 12-inch howitzers mounted on carriages and moved around on railway tracks, which took a long time to dismantle and reposition. It was noisy, dangerous work because the Germans frequently tried to target the teams behind these heavy field guns. Jack, however, was lucky enough to survive the war unscathed.

ARTILLERY IN TRENCH WARFARE

When it became clear in 1915 that the war was going to be relatively static, mainly taking place in trenches, the weaponry changed from light field guns, which couldn't fire heavy-enough shells to be effective against well-fortified trenches, to heavier guns like the howitzer. The German Army's "Big Bertha" was a particularly heavy howitzer, firing high-caliber shells at a steep trajectory that caused maximum destruction on the ground. At first howitzers were pulled into position by teams of horses, but by the final months of the war these had been replaced by tractors. The railway howitzers Jack Fox operated first came into use in March 1916. Tanks were also developed in which men could travel across no-man's-land; first used in the Battle of the Somme in September 1916, they achieved more success at Cambrai in November 1917 and Amiens in 1918. Poor communications at the Front meant there were frequent instances of casualties from so-called friendly fire from these new heavy weapons.

TOP & ABOVE
A 12-inch howitzer (top) and an 8-inch one (above) being fired on the Western Front. They had to be anchored in the ground with tons of earth to counteract the kick they gave when fired.

In late 1918 Jack was in the vicinity of Ypres, a town that had once been home to 20,000 people. As the northernmost point of the Western Front, bulging out into German-held territory, it had been fiercely fought over. The Allies only hung on to it at a cost of 25,000 soldiers and untold numbers of civilians. The Gothic cathedral and 13th-century Cloth Hall were in ruins, and barely a building was left standing. Rats scurried among jagged piles of rubble and fractured trees stood out in relief against the sky. It was against this background that Jack met Rachel Dumortier and their doomed attachment began.

La Poudrière

The Dumortier family lived in Dikkebusch, a small village near Ypres, and worked in the transportation business, taking farmers' produce to market by horse and cart. They stayed in the area during the First Battle of Ypres in October and November 1914, during which British forces retook the town that they referred to as "Wipers," which was easier to pronounce than the French name. After that they dug trenches around the 17th-century ramparts by the Menin Gate, from which they could venture forth to attack the German lines surrounding them on three sides. Food soon became scarce, but the Dumortiers stayed on during the Second Battle of Ypres in April to May 1915, when the German forces released chlorine gas. It must have been terrifying as the huge cloud drifted

BELOW
This iconic image of the devastated town of Ypres, taken in January 1917 shows St Martin's Church and the Cloth Hall in ruins.

across the area, causing those caught up in it to cough and choke, with streaming eyes and burning throats. There was constant bombardment from the heavy weapons, day and night, and many citizens fled to stay with family elsewhere, but the Dumortiers had nowhere else to go at that time.

The Belgian royal family were instrumental in creating a scheme whereby Belgian citizens were evacuated to Bergerac in the South of France in late 1915 and early 1916. A large gunpowder plant called La Poudrière had been established on the River Dordogne, complete with temporary wooden housing, a school, and a 700-bed hospital. There were communal dining rooms for the 8,000 staff, markets where they could buy food, and daycare centers for preschool children. Unable to face another winter of freezing cold, food shortages, and constant shelling, not to mention the threat of more poison-gas attacks, the Dumortiers traveled south by train in December 1915 and were allocated a house in Bergerac, within the factory complex. The two eldest girls, seventeen-year-old Adrienne and sixteen-year-old Rachel, started work at the factory, where their job was to stuff gunpowder into shell casings. From time to time there were loud explosions as shells were tested on a nearby firing range. It can't have been pleasant work for the teenage girls, but it was certainly a valuable contribution to the war effort as La Poudrière was soon producing 10 tons of gunpowder a day.

Adrienne's parents had a large family, with five girls and three boys. They all made new friends in Bergerac, but were fiercely homesick for Dikkebusch and hoped against hope that their house and possessions would have survived the fighting. It was not to be. When they returned in the fall of 1918 they

BELOW
Adrienne (left) along with some friends at La Poudrière, the munitions factory where she worked in Bergerac. None of them wore face masks despite the fact that they were handling gunpowder..

found the area flattened and anything they had left behind gone. In the fields there were rotting corpses. Few amenities survived. At a clearing station in Hazebrouck, the Dumortiers were allocated a house in which they could live during the rebuilding of Ypres and its infrastructure.

Meanwhile Jack Fox, still with a year of his ten-year military service to complete, volunteered to help give proper burials to all the soldiers who lay in the ground where they had fallen, often without so much as a cross to mark the spot. A Chinese labor force had been hired to perform the grisly task of "battlefield clearance." This meant they had to pick up body parts and put them in sacks, while looking for any marks or possessions by which the soldier might be identified. They also searched for the telltale signs of a grave just below the surface: grass that was unnaturally green, greenish-black puddles in shell holes that indicated the liquefaction of underlying tissues, or small bones brought to the surface by rats.

ABOVE
Jack working in Bandaghem Cemetery, on the road between Poperinghe and Ypres, 1919. He took great pride in his work.

Jack's first job was at Bandeghem, a cemetery attached to a field hospital. There had been no time, materials, or manpower to make coffins, so bodies were buried in the bloodstained sheets the men had died in, and it was Jack's job to tidy up, mark, and catalog their graves. It was grim work, but he felt a huge debt of gratitude to these men who had given their lives and he wanted to honor them. Only by a fluke was he still alive while they had perished. He lived in a mobile van with a friend, working as long as there was daylight and cycling to nearby towns to find food and company in the evenings. One evening, at a social club in Hazebrouck, he met Rachel Dumortier, who had found work as a spinner in a textile factory, and her company was a welcome respite from the horror of his day job. Rachel was very pretty and although she only spoke Flemish and French while he spoke only English, they soon fell for each other. Communicating through sign language and the odd words they picked up, the two grew very attached to each other and, according to some family members, began a passionate romance.

> *The two grew very attached to each other and began a passionate romance.*

Laying Down the Law

In early 1919 Jack went home on leave to visit his mother, who now lived in Newark-on-Trent, and he sent a card back to Rachel in Hazebrouck, written in painstaking French, probably with the help of a friend: "It is my desire to come back quickly," he wrote. She had asked him to bring her a dress and he said he didn't know which style she meant, but wrote, "You remain very pretty forever . . . hope you are very content." When he came back, Rachel took Jack home to introduce him to her family, who immediately objected to the relationship. He was twenty-seven and, in the family's opinion, too old for the nineteen-year-old Rachel. Besides, according to tradition the eldest daughter of the family must be married first. The Dumortiers informed Jack in no uncertain terms that he had to marry Adrienne, who was two years older. Plump, with strong features and a domineering nature, she was not nearly as appealing as her younger sister.

Jack was inexperienced with women—Rachel was probably his first girlfriend—so he didn't know what to do when faced with the pressure from this huge extended family. He loved Rachel, but everyone was insisting that he do the right thing, to the extent that

BELOW
The wedding of Adrienne and Jack on November 24, 1919. Rachel is standing behind Adrienne, looking glum but resigned, and their three younger sisters sit in front. None of Jack's family were present.

he was told he would bring shame on the family if he did not concur. At last he caved in and on November 24, 1919, he married Adrienne in a ceremony at Hazebrouck's town hall. Rachel attended, putting a brave face on her heartache and disappointment. So poor was Jack's grasp of Flemish that a translator had to be brought in to translate the wedding vows for him. None of his English family was able to travel over for the ceremony; if they had, perhaps they might have talked him out of it.

Jack and Adrienne moved into a white wooden hut in Dikkebusch, constructed from prefabricated kits brought over from England; they used packing cases for furniture. His army service came to an end, but he still had a period of four years as a reservist and applied for a post with the Imperial War Graves Commission formed in 1919 so that he could continue tending the graveyards in the area. In November 1920, Jack and Adrienne's first child was born—a girl they called Mariejeanne—followed a year later by a stillborn boy. Adrienne always believed the boy's death was caused by the toxic effects of the gunpowder she had inhaled while working in La Poudrière. They had worn overalls and headscarves, but were never given facemasks to protect them from the dangerous chemicals they handled.

On January 4, 1921, there was a further tragedy in the Dumortier family when Rachel suddenly passed away. She'd been hit on the side of the head by a snowball containing a concealed stone and had died of a brain injury. Jack and Adrienne were devastated by the sudden and shocking loss, with Jack mourning the vivacious girl he had loved so dearly. Later that year, he and Adrienne moved to a house on the Chausée de Bruges in Ypres, where they had three more daughters, followed in 1935 by twin boys, one of whom was deprived of oxygen during birth and died the following year. For the rest of her life, Adrienne would carry a picture of his little white coffin wherever she went. A pall of sadness hung over their married life.

There was a thriving British community in the Ypres area, associated with the War Graves Commission, and a British church and school were established, as well as a cricket team. Jack was a kindly father who never raised a hand to his little ones, and he taught at the Anglican Sunday school, bringing up his children in the Anglican faith although their mother was Catholic. The Fox family spoke English at home but Adrienne's accent was described

> *At last he caved in and on November 24, 1919 he married Adrienne ...*

BATTLEFIELD TOURISM

In the week of the 1918 Armistice, Thomas Cook & Son ran an ad in the newspapers promoting trips to the battlefields for those who had lost loved ones and wanted to see their graves. However, those who did rush out on tours were distressed to find the poor state of the graveyards, with little documentation to help them track down individual graves. By 1919, Thomas Cook offered two tours: a luxury option for £36.75, and a more basic option for about £10—this in an era when the average wage was £3 a week. The YMCA opened a 40-bed hostel in Ypres in August 1919, and the extended Dumortier family got involved in transporting tourists to the battlefields by taxi before going on to start their own local bus service. The industry grew over the decades and museums sprang up catering for those interested in the region's history as well as those making a pilgrimage to the grave of a loved one or searching among the 54,896 names inscribed on the Menin Gate of casualties whose bodies have never been found.

as sounding "like broken Welsh," and when she was cross with her children she would tell them off in Flemish. The Dumortier children received a good education and lived comfortably because Jack's salary was paid in sterling at a time when the exchange rate was favorable, but the marriage was strained. Adrienne was an argumentative woman and Jack, who did not like quarreling, would often retort during arguments, "You are a nail in my coffin." It was a strange kind of life, in a patriotic British enclave right in the heart of Belgian territory surrounded by cemeteries and memorials to the dead.

Surviving Another War

In 1939, after war was declared yet again, most British citizens of Ypres remained where they were as no one could contemplate a repeat of the 1914–18 war when the town had been under siege. Less than a year later, however, in May 1940, Jack, Adrienne, and their children were forced to leave when the German Blitzkrieg quickly overran the Low Countries. They made a rapid cross-country escape along with 300 other

ABOVE
A branch of the Dumortier family in Poperinghe opened a bus company after the war. Battlefield tourism made an important contribution to the post-war economy of the region.

British residents of Ypres,
sleeping in barns by night
while German bombs rained
all around them, before
finally getting on board
a cargo ship, *The City of
Christchurch,* at Calais on
May 24, which took them
to Southampton.

The Fox family settled
in Burnt Oak, North London,
where Jack took a job
delivering machine tools to
factories on his motorbike, and also worked
as a nightwatchman for a factory making
aircraft parts. There was no question that
they would stay in England after the war
ended, though, because Adrienne missed
her parents, brothers, and sisters, who were
all still in Belgium. The family returned early
in 1946, and Jack went back to his work in
the war cemeteries.

In 1952, Adrienne died from complications
resulting from diabetes and, as they
followed her black horse-drawn hearse
down the street, her daughter Betty
remarked to her surviving son Jimmy,
"It's all over, thank God." For decades their
parents had endured a marriage they were
forced into and their children had been
witnesses to the tension this had caused. After Adrienne's death,
Jack brought Jimmy and Betty back to Burnt Oak, where he lived
for the remainder of his life, working contentedly as a gardener at
a hospital and nurses' training school.

Jack was a good man and would never have left his wife. All
the evidence is that their love for each other grew through the
years of marriage and raising children, but Adrienne must always
have resented the fact that he had loved her sister Rachel first and
foremost. Their marriage, lived out among the graves of the war
dead, was haunted by her memory.

ABOVE
*Jimmy and Jack Fox
around 1950. Jimmy is
wearing the Ypres British
Memorial School cap.*

TOP
*Adrienne holding her
twin boys, Jimmy and
John; John would die
before his first birthday.*

ACKNOWLEDGMENTS

The account of Evelyn and Frederick Albright and extracts of their correspondence are from *An Echo in my Heart: The Letters of Elnora Evelyn (Kelly) Albright and Frederick Stanley Albright,* compiled and edited by Lorna Brooke. Many thanks to Lorna for permission to quote from them. You can read them at www.echoinmyheart.ca. Letters and material pertaining to the Albright collection are housed in The Archives and Research Collections Centre in the D.B. Weldon Library at Western University, London, Ontario, Canada.

Warm thanks to Charles Merrill, grandson of Charlie and Valentine Boucher, for allowing me to quote from his grandfather's war memoirs and for answering my other questions about them as well as sending photographs. His website is www.luckycharlie.com

I heard Jack and Adrienne Fox's story directly from their son Jimmy Fox and I am extremely grateful to him for all the time spent on the telephone with me and for the long emails full of information as well as dozens of photographs. I recommend his book *The Children Who Fought Hitler* (London: John Murray, 2010) for the compelling story of the British community in Ypres. Thanks also to Dominiek Dendhooven of the Flanders Field Museum in Ypres for putting us in touch and making many other helpful suggestions.

For information on Ivor Gurney's romance with Annie Drummond, one of the best sources is Pamela Blevins's excellent book *Ivor Gurney and Marion Scott: Song of Pain and Beauty* (Suffolk: Boydell Press, 2008).

The letters of Hugh Wallace and Jessie Mann are reproduced in *Under the Shadow: Letters of Love and War 1911–1917*, compiled and edited by Brid Hetherington (Dunfermline: Cuallan Press, 1999). I'm very grateful to her for permission to quote from them, for sending photographs, and for all her help. Letters and photographs of the Manns are housed in Glasgow University Archive, Glasgow, UK.

Grateful thanks to Máire Uí Éafa, daughter-in-law of Joseph and Mary Heapes, for answering my questions and digging out old family photographs. Thanks also to Eleanor Kenny at the British Library for putting us in touch.

Rebecca Cazares and Jeff Staley kindly gave me permission to quote from the letters of their grandfather Lloyd Maywood Staley to Mary Beatrice Gray. Their very interesting website is at www.u.arizona. edu/~rstaley/wwlettr1.htm

The story of Max Ernst's relationship with Luise Straus is beautifully told in their son Jimmy Ernst's book *A Not-So-Still Life* (New York: Pushcart Press, 1984). I'm grateful to Dr Jürgen Pech of the Max Ernst Museum in Brühl, Germany, for information on Max Ernst's war career,

Acknowledgments

and to Isabel Varea for help with German to English translation.

Jacqui Smythe kindly agreed to let me quote from Percy Smythe's letters and diaries, which are reproduced on her very informative website about the whole Smythe family at www.smythe.id.au. It is well worth visiting as it also contains the love stories of Percy's brothers Vern and Viv.

For more information on Agnes von Kurowsky's relationship with Ernest Hemingway, I highly recommend Henry S. Villard and James Nagel's *Hemingway in Love and War* (New York: Hyperion, 1989), which reproduces her diary and some of their letters to each other. They are now held in the archive Agnes Von Kurowsky Personal Papers/John F. Kennedy Presidential Library and Museum, Boston.

For more on Robert Digby and Claire Dessenne, and for a cracking good mystery story as well as a description of life in wartime France, see Ben Macintyre's *A Foreign Field* (London: HarperPress, 2010).

Edward J. Renehan Jr.'s book *The Lion's Pride: Theodore Roosevelt and his Family in Peace and War* (Oxford: Oxford University Press, 1998) was a useful source for the story of Quentin Roosevelt and Flora Payne Whitney.

Humphrey Carpenter's *J.R.R. Tolkien: A Biography* (New York: Houghton Mifflin, 2000) provides a balanced, very readable look at the life of the Tolkiens.

D. Bruce Cherry gave me lots of leads when I was starting out on this book and Colin Salter helped me to track down some of the couples. Thanks, guys!

Huge thanks as always to the wonderful team at Ivy Press: Sophie Collins, Jayne Ansell, Katie Greenwood, Wayne Blades, and Andrew Milne.

And thanks to Karel for being Karel.

PICTURE CREDITS

Thank you to all of the individuals and collections who supplied images:

Albright and Kelly Family Fonds, Western Archives, Western University: *2*TR, *2*TL, *92, 93, 94, 95, 96, 97, 98, 98, 100, 101*T, *103*.

The Art Archive: *116*B, *161*; Archives Charmet: *53*; Imperial War Museum: *159*; Private Collection Newbury: *51*; Amoret Tanner Collection: *104*B.

Birmingham Archives: *105, 106*.

From the private collection of Pieter Collier, www.tolkienlibrary.com: *152*B, *163*.

Corbis/American Red Cross/National Geographic Society: *87*; Bettmann: *87*.

John Fawkes, www.britishbattles.com: *20*T.

Fotolia: *121*.

Courtesy of Jimmy Fox: *176*T, *177, 178, 179, 182, 183, 184, 186, 187*.

Getty Images/Hulton Archive: *130*T, *181*; Imperial War Museum: *113*; Popperfoto: *124*; Science & Society Picture Library: *78*; Time & Life Pictures: *14, 162*T; Topical Press Agency: *147*; Universal Images Group: *52*.

Ivor Gurney Collection, Gloucestershire Archives © The Ivor Gurney Estate: *32*T, *32*R, *33*R, *34, 37, 38*T, *39, 41, 42*.

Ernest Hemingway Collection, John F. Kennedy Presidential Library and Museum, Boston: *81, 82, 83, 84, 86, 88, 89, 90*.

Courtesy of Brid Hetherington: *105, 106, 108, 109, 110, 114, 115*.

Library and Archives Canada: *101*B, *102*.

Library of Congress, Washington D.C: *6, 7, 8, 10, 11, 12, 13, 15, 16, 17, 18, 19, 30*B, *44*T, *48, 61, 64, 65, 72, 73, 77*B, *80, 85, 99, 126, 134*T, *142, 143, 144, 145, 146, 148, 151, 158, 169, 170*B, *173, 180*B.

Mary Evans Picture Library/David Cohen Fine Art: *160*; Epic: *157*; Epic/Tallandier: *38*B, *54*; The Everett Collection: *119*; John Frost Newspapers: *137*; Grenville Collins

Postcard Collection: *74*; Peter Higginbotham Collection: *75*; Robert Hunt Collection/ Imperial War Museum: *40*; Robert Hunt Library: *49, 112, 132, 180*T; Interfoto: *50*; Pump Park Photography: *111*; Sueddeutsche Zeitung Photo: *9*; ©Thomas Cook Archive: *176*B; westernfrontphotography.com: *162*B.

Peggy Ann McKay Carter: *33*L.

Courtesy of Charles Merrill, www. luckycharlie.com: *69, 70, 77*T, *79*.

National Media Museum/Frank Hurley/ Australian War Records Section: *125*.

Oakville Images: *47*.

Courtesy of Jürgen Pech/Max Ernst Museum Brühl des LVR/Foundation Max Ernst: *45, 46*.

Maud Powell Society for Music and Education: Pamela Blevins: *35*.

Rama: *152*T.

William Ready Division of Archives and Research Collections, McMaster University Library, Hamilton, Canada: *56, 57, 58, 59, 62, 63, 66*T, *67*.

Theodore Roosevelt Digital Library, Dickinson State University: *140, 141, 149, 150*.

Shutterstock: *2*BR, *20*B, *44*B, *66*B, *68*B, *68*T, *164*B.

© Smythe Family, www.smythe.id.au. Courtesy of Jacqui Kennedy: *116*T, *117, 118, 120, 122, 123*.

Courtesy of Jeff Staley: *2*B, *164*T, *165, 166, 167, 170*T, *174, 175*.

Topfoto: *133, 134*B; Pamela Chandler/ ArenaPAL: *153, 154*; Charles Walker: *25*.

Courtesy of Máire Uí Éafa: *128, 129, 130*B, *131, 135, 136, 138, 139*.

Every effort has been made to trace copyright holders and acknowledge the pictures in this publication. We apologize if there are any unintentional omissions, and welcome information so that future editions can be updated.